Physical Education Activities

Marjorie Sutcliffe

Bright Ideas
FOR Early Years

Published by Scholastic Ltd
Villiers House, Clarendon Avenue,
Leamington Spa,
Warwickshire CV32 5PR

© 1993 Scholastic Ltd
4567890   67890123

Written by Marjorie Sutcliffe
Edited by Catherine Bywater
Sub-edited by Sophie Jowett
Designed by Micky Pledge
Illustrations by Francis Scapaticci
Cover design by Lynne Joesbury
Cover photograph by Fiona Pragoff

Photographs by Sally and Richard
Greenhill (pages 5 and 57), Chris Kelly
(page 13), Bob Bray (page 21), Marjorie
Sutcliffe (page 31), Garry Clarke (page
39), David Johnson (pages 49 and 65),
Insight (page 77)

Artwork by Liz Preece, Castle Graphics,
Kenilworth

Typeset by Typesetters (Birmingham) Ltd
Printed in Great Britain by The Alden
Press Ltd, Oxford

British Library Cataloguing in Publication Data
A catalogue record for this book is available from the British
Library

ISBN 0-590-53094-1

Contents

Acknowledgements
A special thank you to Barbara and Sue
at University College Scarborough for
their enthusiastic support and advice, and
to Beverley for all her generous help
and sustaining encouragement.

Introduction

Young children delight in physical activity. They seek out experiences which capture their interest, channel their energies, stimulate their imagination and give them pleasurable sensations. Activities such as running, climbing, balancing, rolling over and skipping are a source of immense satisfaction to them. Children watch and try to copy the actions of others; repeating and 'showing off' their new-found skills are important in developing self-confidence and self-esteem.

Children use movement to express themselves and to act out rhymes and stories. The foundations for all basic movement patterns are laid down in these early years, so children need plenty of opportunities to experience and practise a wide range of movements. Regular exercise is essential in helping young bodies become strong, flexible and well co-ordinated. School can do much to foster and extend children's love of action, helping them to become safe, confident and imaginative movers.

Learning about movement

Children enjoy being active and responding to movement challenges with increasing confidence and success. They need positive feedback on their activities, and, as movement abilities are displayed so publicly, this is particularly important to them. Success or failure when catching a ball, reaching the top of the climbing frame or jumping a turning rope are significant experiences for young children. Apart from personal satisfaction, they are motivated to progress further when their achievements are recognised and reinforced by others.

By testing themselves in a range of situations well-matched to their own needs, children begin to delight in, and explore further, their own physical capabilities. They learn to trust their own bodies and know when it is safe to take a risk.

Learning through movement

Movement is a sensory-rich, fully integrated experience involving thought, action and sensation. Many concepts can be more fully understood when movement forms an intrinsic part of the learning process. For example, children experience forces as they push a heavily loaded trolley up a slope, then try to control it as it runs down again.

Physical play helps children to socialise and extend their language. They share equipment, take turns, show each other actions, look out for each other's safety and actively co-operate.

Equality of access and opportunity

All children should benefit from taking part in physical activities. There should be no barriers to access or opportunity based on race, culture, gender or ability.

Young children will have had varying movement opportunities and experiences before starting school, and many will need time to feel 'at home' in the larger area before they begin to move around with confidence. They need time to pace their own play, and encouragement to join in and repeat enjoyable activities before extending their range of movements. As well as equal access, both boys and girls should have equal opportunities to participate in a wide range of activities.

Choice and structure

The degree of structure planned by the teacher and the amount of choice given to children in both the equipment and the activity can vary. A sample planning sheet can be found on photocopiable page 93. This may mean:
● children being free to choose from equipment on offer, usually directing their own activity with the adults encouraging, supporting and extending that activity;
● children choosing to opt into an activity which is structured by the teacher;
● a set group of children using a range of equipment chosen by the teacher with which to direct their own activity;
● a set group of children working with equipment and activities chosen and structured by the teacher.

Three- and four-year-olds will often be free to choose from the activities and equipment on offer, but later a more structured focus to activities can be given to small groups or individuals.

Five- and six-year-olds should have the opportunity to participate in a structured and well-balanced programme of physical education. However, opportunities to choose freely from equipment on offer should still form some part of a broad and balanced physical education experience for all children under seven.

Space and equipment

Children need:
● a safe outdoor space;
● a safe indoor space;
● large outdoor and indoor equipment for activities requiring strength, balance, agility, judgement;
● portable equipment for a range of purposes, such as construction and role-play;
● small equipment for practising hand/eye and foot/eye co-ordination;
● percussion, audio system and tapes/CDs.

Individual differences

Children vary in physique, strength, co-ordination, confidence and movement judgement. In these early stages some will be energetic and exuberant movers, while others will be hesitant, lacking in confidence and concerned about getting hurt. A good 'match' will focus on providing a range of activities which take into account previous experiences or lack of them and current 'needs'. It will encourage children to meet new challenges with confidence by taking part in activities just beyond their present level of attainment. However, it must be remembered that children also need to enjoy the security which familiar activities and equipment provide.

Differentiation

Effective planning takes into account the individual differences among children — vital when physical challenge, risk and body movement are involved. Differentiation can be made on the basis of task or outcome. This will depend on the physical and cognitive demands of the activity and the range of equipment available.

Children may be grouped according to ability, for example, when running fast over short distances; or different groups may be given different tasks as in swimming.

Children may be given a common task, but providing a variety of equipment will encourage them to select appropriately from different types of equipment, for instance, balls of different sizes and textures. Tables of varying heights will give all children the opportunity to jump down and land safely.

Differentiation often comes through outcome, with a range of movement responses resulting from one task. For example, an activity based on rolling in different shapes may result in some children stretching out and rolling over sideways, while others will be curling up small and rolling over sideways, backwards or forwards. Children work at their own level and pace; the teacher's role is to encourage and provide individual guidance.

Special educational needs

There are some children who have special educational needs (as defined under the 1981 Education Act), but not in the area of physical education. There may be other children who have special educational needs in physical activities. Teachers need to be informed about the individual children's needs and their implications for learning in a range of physical activities.

Entitlement, access, integration and integrity

All children are entitled to become involved in, and have access to, the full range of physical education activities, modified where necessary. Inclusion rather than exclusion is crucial. Whenever possible, children with special needs should be integrated with the rest of the group and given additional help, if necessary. Any modified activities should have integrity and real learning potential for the child — they must not be seen as trivial 'time-fillers'.

Children who are identified as having mild or moderate learning difficulties may need the task broken down into a sequence of achievable steps. This may relate to the instructions being given or to the nature of the task itself. For example, walking along a narrow surface requires confidence, a sense of position, muscular control, careful placement of the feet and good co-ordination of sight, touch and sense of balance.

Communicating instructions in a clear and well-ordered manner is important. The child must understand the task and the sequenced pattern of movements needed in order to be successful. Children with physical disabilities or general movement problems need to be involved in activities which help them to extend their own movement abilities in as wide a range of actions as possible.

Advice should be sought on the needs of individual children. There will be children who are gifted in a particular activity. They need to nurture their talent, both inside and outside the school, but need also to participate in a broad and balanced range of activities in these early years.

This book does not claim to cater for children with severe and/or multiple learning difficulties. Outside help should be sought in planning appropriate physical activities for their individual needs.

Safety

Concern for children's safety is essential at all times. All physical activities involve some risk and the degree of risk in any movement needs to be assessed carefully by anticipating children's movements. Minimising risk while retaining the thrill of the challenge is an important balance to strive for. Ground rules about play spaces, activities and the use of equipment must be laid down and understood by all the children, who should be encouraged to take responsibility for their own actions. Only by 'doing', in physical play and in more structured physical education activities, do young children come to assess risk for themselves and learn to move safely.

Supporting and extending children's learning

High expectations

Have high expectations of all the children, while valuing each one for his or her unique individuality. Encourage and reinforce good quality in all they do, from folding clothes tidily as they change to listening carefully and practising hard to improve a pattern of jumps. Recognise and praise children's efforts as they try out, select, improve and extend their movements.

Observation

Movement is fleeting so permanent records of children's movements are rare. The teacher's observation skills are the key to effective teaching and learning. Focusing observation on the specific demands of the activity will help in checking whether the 'match' of child and activity is appropriate. Observation may focus on a child's safety skills, for example, when rolling over, or it may focus on her co-ordination skills as she catches a bouncing ball. In some cases, the task or the equipment will need to be modified. Careful observation will help to give effective guidance to individual children, as well as form the basis for future planning.

Encouragement and intervention

Once children are actively involved, they need adults to show an interest in their movements. Watch them and give verbal reassurance and encouragement. Once children become more familiar with the equipment or the activity, it is important to focus attention on helping them to become more controlled. Much practice and repetition is essential for effective patterns of movement to be established. Later on, extend practice across a variety of situations; this helps children to adapt movements to the changing situation.

At times, you may need to intervene to prevent a hazardous activity from being repeated. When you do this, explain to children why this was necessary and check that further attempts show necessary modification.

Physical support

Children should be able to solve their own movement problems; the demands of the task should never be too far beyond their current achievement. Apart from being close by, for example, to hold a child's hand to walk a balance bar for the first time, you should rarely need to offer physical support.

Choice is necessary where physical risk is a feature of the activity. Children need to make sensible choices based on their current abilities and limitations. However, they do need to practise basic skills like climbing, landing and rolling and to understand the implications for safety.

About the book

This book offers ideas for planning physical activities across a range of movement experiences. Children are encouraged to become actively involved in planning and modifying their own movements as they perform. All young children need to experience a range of activities which lead to athletics, dance, games, gymnastics and outdoor challenges.

11

Many of the ideas in the book can be adapted to suit different situations and type of equipment available. Careful selection should enable almost all children to become involved and to achieve. Within each chapter, the ideas cover a range of the key features of the activity area. Each idea has a particular learning focus and places certain demands on the child. In general, the later ideas in each chapter make more demands than the earlier ones. Some of the activities are more suited for use with a small group of children, but many can be used with larger groups.

Early activity is divided into the following sections:
• 'Objective' identifies the learning focus for the activity;
• 'What you need' suggests a range of equipment which will meet the needs of most children within the group;
• 'What to do' indicates ways in which children can be involved in the activity.
• 'What to look for' offers ideas for observing children's movement and supporting their learning. These often identify the key demands on the children as they plan, perform and modify their movements. Observations should be matched with appropriate descriptions and questioning. Children will observe and copy the movements of others as they play, with more structured opportunities to 'show and share' ideas involving the whole group.
• 'Follow-up' gives further ideas for extending the activity.

Timing activities

The ideas will involve young children for varying lengths of time. Some are very energetic, like 'Treacle' (see page 42), and may only last two or three minutes, but can be returned to later on in the session. Others like 'Stations' (see page 48) provide a format for a full session or, with variations, for many sessions. As a general rule, provide a balance of activities: short bursts of energetic ones contrasted with those requiring more careful control.

Getting started

Chapter one

Have a look at the spaces which are used or could be used for physical activity. The potential of each area needs to be explored fully so that children are involved in physical activities on a regular basis. It may well be the case that existing spaces could offer a greater variety of opportunities for active play than they do at present.

Inside the nursery

A permanent space is ideal, but the balance between physical activity and safety must be assessed in each situation. It is useful to have a space which can be cleared for action rhymes, music and movement. Opportunities to build with large construction units and to practise other motor skills, like balancing, may be possible at certain times indoors.

Outside the nursery

The outdoor area is important. It needs to look attractive and to stimulate children into activity. Almost all nurseries have a paved yard which provide three- and four-year-old children with a safe space in which they can run around freely and use portable equipment, such as wheeled toys and balls. There should be some equipment, fixed or portable, for children to practise climbing, swinging, hanging and balancing skills.

A grassy area, preferably including an undulating surface, will provide many opportunities for physical play. Slopes and mounds are good for physical exertion such as running up and down, rolling down and for pushing and pulling loads.

If some natural features, like bushes, or tree stumps in the grass, are available, so much the better. Boundaries must be well-maintained and the playing area kept secure.

Fixed equipment

This provides an exciting challenge for children, encouraging them to climb up, along, over and down and to hang, swing, balance and slide. Professional advice should be sought in selecting and siting any fixed equipment in the space available. Equipment should be as 'multi-purpose' as possible, encouraging a wide variety of actions and providing different levels of challenge. The equipment should not dominate the play space to such an extent that it restricts the range of other outdoor play activities.

Portable equipment

Portable equipment can also provide valuable opportunities for climbing, balancing, jumping and sliding. This type can often be assembled in a variety of ways to cater for children with varying levels of confidence and competence, as well as for encouraging different actions.

Smaller equipment for use outdoors includes tyres, barrels, tunnels, see-saws, houses, wheeled toys, balls, hoops and large building units. Some equipment will be set up beforehand, but other things, like hoops and skittles, can be positioned for the children to collect and arrange for themselves. It is useful to have times when only certain items are available, like balls, particularly if space is limited. At other times, set up the equipment in a way which will stimulate and extend work on other activities, like homes and buildings.

Safety check

A visual safety check of equipment must be made every day for signs of wear and tear and damage. Keep a look out for any signs of vandalism or rubbish which may have been thrown into the play area, for example, dog dirt or glass, and for the general condition of playing surfaces and equipment. If there are any doubts about a piece of equipment, remove it from use immediately until it can be repaired. If this is difficult, make sure that it presents no danger to the children; immobilise or place some protection around the damaged equipment.

The infant playground/field

Playtime

The playground should be an inviting area in which children can spend their time happily. However, experiences at playtime can be far from enjoyable for some children and can sometimes compare unfavourably with those they experienced outdoors in the nursery. It can be difficult to manage a large number of children with different needs, playing in an area which provides little positive stimulus, and this can create a range of behavioural problems.

A review of the play space including its layout, current use and provision of equipment alongside the drawing up of playground rules can go some way to making playtime a happier and more enjoyable period for children and adults alike. Children's concerns and ideas are an important part of this review and must be valued.

Extending movement opportunities

Is there some fixed or small equipment available for the children to use when they are playing outside? If space prevents the use of equipment like balls and ropes, or means that one activity tends to dominate, then divide up the area.

It is useful to have some portable climbing equipment available which can be brought into the infant playground or onto grass for the younger children to use. It can provide important opportunities to practise and extend their climbing, hanging, swinging and sliding skills as well as being a stimulus for imaginative play. Some infant gymnastic apparatus can be daunting for cautious children who have little previous experience. They need time to practise and pace their own activity before their confidence can grow.

P.E. sessions

Most energetic activities, particularly those in which games equipment is used and running is involved, are best done out of doors, on a hard surface or on grass. The playing area can be marked off easily using cones, multi-markers or even bean bags.

Using a hall space

Hall time is usually fixed, so aim to be in there for the maximum amount of time during each session, with the children active for as much time as possible. Establish a clear code of working rules for P.E. with high expectations of children's responses, so sessions are enjoyable, purposeful and, above all, safe.

With groups of younger children

If there is a hall available, consider taking a group of children to visit it. Even in the early stages an infant hall can be used very happily by groups of three- and four-year-olds for physical activity. This should be seen as valuable in its own right, and not merely as a preparation for P.E. sessions later on. Playing in only part of the area, enclosed by a screen, can help make a small group feel more secure initially.

The hall can be used for play with suitable games equipment, for action rhymes, for dancing and for gymnastic activities with or without low apparatus. If the hall is heavily used by other classes, try to negotiate having some time in there during one of the school's morning playtimes, if it is free.

With classes of older children

As most of the P.E. sessions will take place in the hall for five- and six-year-olds and for some groups of four-year-olds, careful planning and organisation is essential so children get a balanced physical experience.

Organising equipment

Equipment needs to be well organised and stored tidily so that access to it is easy. Any heavy portable apparatus which is used regularly should be kept as near as possible to its point of use in the hall.

Games equipment can be stored in boxes with handles. It is useful to have either boxes of mixed equipment (for example, balls, ropes, bean bags, plastic rackets and sticks of the same colour) or boxes of the same type of equipment (like bean bags) kept together. Label each box with its contents.

Much of the equipment can be arranged around the playing space and children can be encouraged to see and remember where each piece of equipment is stored and be responsible for its careful return.

Clothes for physical activity

Younger children

Children need to wear comfortable clothes which allow freedom of movement. For outdoor play, tracksuit-type tops and trousers are ideal with soft soled, well-fitting shoes such as trainers. In warm weather, T-shirts and shorts should be enouraged outdoors.

If groups go into a hall, it may be best if children only take off jumpers and shoes and socks or tights at first, but this depends on the type of physical activity. If low gymnastic apparatus is used, it will be necessary also to remove trousers and skirts.

Older children

If the floor is suitable in the school hall, children can work in bare feet for gymnastics and dance and wear only vests and pants. Soft soled, light plimsolls need to be worn for games activities where children are moving and stopping more quickly and controlling balls with their feet. Stockinged feet and long trousers cause children to slip and slide, and should not be worn. For outdoor sessions children should wear comfortable clothing which is neither restrictive nor too loose.

Getting changed
If children get fully changed for their physical activity, give them plenty of time so they are ready by the start time. A sand timer is useful to speed up older groups. No jewellery should be worn for any physical activity; this should be removed and stored safely. Some children will need help in the early stages but encourage them to turn clothes the right way out and fold them neatly with socks placed inside shoes, and shoes left side by side, left then right.

Avoid having children queueing by the door for several minutes until everyone is ready as they can easily become restless. One way is to gather them on the carpet as they become ready and to play a familiar action game with them, or have one child act as a leader for a 'copy me' type activity.

The P.E. session

Purposeful activity

Although the emphasis in each lesson will vary, all sessions should have a real 'physical' dimension. It is important to set and maintain a good pace as children need and enjoy the exhilaration of action, not sitting and listening for long periods. Avoid long explanations or showing too many individual demonstrations at any one time.

Hold children's attention with a concise introduction, followed by a burst of activity. Stop the activity to re-direct children's attention when necessary. Showing an example of a successful response to a task is often useful in re-channelling their energies after a period of practice.

Pattern of the session

Most sessions will have three or four parts. A sample planning sheet is given on photocopiable page 94.

A starter activity
This should last for a couple of minutes to develop listening skills and encourage children to 'tune in' to their body, and to prepare for more thoughtful and vigorous work.

The main activity
This (or these if there is more than one) follows and has a clear learning focus. Plan to follow an energetic activity with a quieter one. For example, moving around contrasted with being on the spot or jumping contrasted with balancing.

A calming final activity
This helps to 'quieten' the body and to re-focus the children's attention.

Sharing the session focus with the group

Select the focus for the activity/session and share it with the children at the start. It helps to have them sitting close by you at this stage. You may need to remind them about the 'one at a time' rule, how to find different ways of controlling a ball with their feet or to practise quiet landings. Helping children to work independently is important and they can be encouraged to plan out and talk about their own work.

At the end of a session, find time to share a few of your observations with the children as a group, recognising individual effort and achievement.

Responding to the teacher

Children should understand that they must work quietly at all times. They must listen for your voice and respond to it as quickly as it is safe to do so. If a problem occurs, like misuse of equipment or unacceptable behaviour, try to deal with it on an individual basis. In the early stages, however, there will be times when situations need to be talked through with the whole group. Explain why an action should be performed in a safer way and give the children a positive focus for further practice. In a larger space you may need to exaggerate your facial expression and the tone of your voice to communicate messages of praise, encouragement and disapproval.

A code for safe, sensible working

Each playing space has its own particular advantages and disadvantages. From the start, children should be helped to feel secure and confident in their play space, while being made aware of any specific hazards. They must be enouraged to move with their own and other children's safety in mind.

Rules, such as working very quietly and responding to signals, should be explained clearly so children understand why they are needed. Children should be encouraged to get involved in the safe practice of any activity – for example noticing that safety catches are in place and returning stray balls to their storage area.

The use of demonstrations

In a secure atmosphere, almost all young children enjoy sharing their movements with others. Demonstrations are invaluable for reinforcing and illustrating the task after a short practice. They reward effort and invention and they are vital for encouraging high quality work. Try to ensure that all children have a chance to share their work with the group at some time.

Always focus the children's observation on one feature of a child's movement or look at similarities or differences in two responses to a task. The quality of children's movements is often considerably higher just after watching a demonstration.

In case of accidents

All physical activity involves risk. The most carefully organised and well-matched series of activities can still result in a child being injured accidently. Teachers have a 'duty of care' to the children and any accidents should be *unforeseen*, and not as a result of a failure to anticipate the risk involved in a particular activity. In case of an emergency, you should be familiar with the school's accident policy and the procedure for administering first aid. If in doubt, seek advice from the LEA or other professional body.

Outdoor physical play

Chapter two

Playing outside, under an ever-changing sky, with natural light, fresh air and in different weather is of value in its own right. Having a safe outdoor space in which children can run around and play with a range of equipment is very important. Although the outdoors is, in general, an integral part of the total learning environment, it offers specific opportunities for children to enjoy practising many physical skills and to satisfy their sense of adventure. Through imaginative play, children will engage in experiences which assist in many areas of their development.

However, learning to move safely and confidently should have high status. Opportunities to use and extend a range of physical skills need to be on offer so children can select equipment to initiate and develop their own physical play. Sometimes the physical activity may be done for its own sake, like jumping off steps; at other times it may be done as part of a game or in imaginative play, like being on board a ship.

The outdoor area

Whatever the size of the outdoor area or its surface, it should be made as attractive and inviting as possible. Are there any unsightly parts of the area? Can any bare walls be brightened up? Are there stimulating markings on the ground? If the space is large, are there any natural features in the space, like bushes or logs, which can be used to divide it up? Bushes in tubs provide flexibility, but choose features which will stimulate activities, like running around or jumping on and off. Low walls can be used for a range of activities. Check that the storage area is secure with all equipment inside well organised, so it can be collected easily.

Access to the outdoors

Ideally, there needs to be a door from the indoors space leading directly and safely to the outdoor space with children having access to it at any time. This can only occur if the outdoor space is constantly supervised. In a nursery area this is usually easier than in an infant area where only one adult may be with the group for much of the time. If this is the case, try to plan times, other than at playtime, when you can take the full group into the playground. If there is another trained adult with the group for part of the time, this could provide a useful opportunity to take small groups outside.

Focus on physical development

The type of equipment and materials made available for children in outdoor play will determine, to a large extent, the range of physical activities which take place. Children will usually make their own decisions about what equipment they need for their play, solving the movement problems they meet in their own way. Adults need to observe and intervene as necessary to help individual children make progress.

Young children need opportunities for:

- physical involvement;
- problem solving in movement;
- enjoyment and achievement;
- learning to trust their own body;
- learning to assess risk and make decisions about their own actions;
- energetic running and chasing in safety;
- lower body strength development from jumping, skipping, hopping, scrambling;
- upper body strength development from climbing, swinging, pulling and pushing, twisting, bending, lifting;
- improving control and co-ordination;
- co-operating with others in activities;
- using physical skills;
- using physical abilities in imaginative play.

Equipment

Quality

Equipment needs to engage children fully, stimulating them to explore and create, and direct their own learning. Simplicity in design is often an advantage, as it allows for more imaginative use. Choose well-designed equipment which is constructed from durable materials. Fixed playground equipment should comply with current recognised standards, for example, British Standard 5696. Equipment needs to survive the rigours of constant use in all weathers. Wheeled toys, like trucks and trolleys, encourage co-operative play if they are generously proportioned.

Range

A range of equipment and materials to assist physical development is listed on page 92.

Water play

Apart from enjoying and exploring the properties of water using a water table and objects or buckets, some groups of children may have the opportunity to use a portable paddling pool or to visit a larger learner pool. Ensuring the health and safety of each child is essential, and specific details concerning filling, using, emptying and cleaning of a paddling pool is outside the scope of this book. Advice should be sought from the Local Authority on these matters and on the level of support and supervision necessary when children are in water.

Imaginative play

All the equipment listed will often be used for imaginative play. Wheeled toys may be lorries, buses or fire engines and the climbing frame may be a 'pretend' building site or a ship. However, children will still be using physical skills whatever function the equipment is serving. The potential for movement can often be extended when imaginative play is the focus. For example, loading and transporting boxes or 'bricks' to the building site, then working out how many can be pushed up a slope in a wheelbarrow to the 'scaffolding'.

Challenge and adventure

Children need to be drawn towards and stimulated into activity by the way equipment is positioned and combined together; they should find it neither too daunting nor too lacking in challenge. As children are at different stages in their physical development, the equipment should reflect variation in challenge too. Having platforms at different heights to jump from, stepping stones set at varying distances apart and access to a range of balls all help children to choose equipment which meets their current needs. The more tentative child needs to feel secure with equipment, while the more adventurous, skilful child will enjoy being extended more fully.

Planning the provision

In fine weather some indoor activities, like painting, can be transferred outside quite naturally, and the local environment itself is a rich resource for learning. Some outdoor activities will not, by their nature, generate much physical activity, so consider the range of opportunities provided during one session or over several sessions. Children need a balanced range of physical experiences.

Choose the range and type of equipment which will be available for the children to use during each session, some of which should have real potential for developing their physical skills. At times this will mean providing just one type of equipment, like a range of balls. At other times there will be a much wider provision of equipment which gives more opportunity for free choice in a range of activities.

Decide where the equipment can be positioned for safety or where it can be collected from by the children. The siting of certain objects of equipment too near each other may create a hazard, so try to anticipate children's likely movement responses. Site items for the more boisterous, energetic activities away from the quieter ones. Children normally move from one piece to another by the most direct route, so try to anticipate probable collision points beforehand and minimise them. The way in which equipment is arranged will suggest and stimulate different ideas for activities; in particular, linking physical play with imaginative play. In order that one activity does not dominate and interfere with another, limit the time or place for use of some equipment, like balls or wheeled toys.

Safe practice

A code of safe working practice for outdoor play needs to be established and understood by all those involved. The amount and quality of supervision and involvement with the children should be at least of the same level as it is indoors.

Some key points

- Children's clothing must allow freedom of movement, with no loose or trailing parts which might get caught on equipment.
- Sturdy footwear is recommended, with a good grip, and which can be securely fastened.
- Observation of children in all parts of the area is essential.
- Rules controlling numbers on certain equipment may be needed.
- Encourage and reinforce acceptable behaviour and appropriate use of equipment.

Role of the adults

Adults have an active role when working outdoors with children, facilitating their learning and interacting with them as they play. Watch children, listen to them and talk with them. At times imaginative play may be the focus, at others the physical features of the play will be an obvious source of attention. You may need to intervene, initiate or join in an activity with an individual or with a group. Or you may wish to observe from a distance, respecting children's need for privacy. Some children need encouragement, reassurance and suggestions to stimulate and direct their play. You will notice the form that their play takes, but note also whether any

individuals show particular difficulties in physical actions like running, balancing and low level climbing, or have any obvious sight, hearing or spatial judgement difficulties when outdoors.

Delight in children's accomplishments and intervene to help their movements become safer by making specific comments. Compliment children who take turns and show awareness of others, and discourage children from showing off or being excessively noisy. Be careful not to distract children when they are concentrating on a difficult movement. Some children may need to have their energies re-directed if they are placing themselves or other children at risk or behaving in an unacceptable way.

Sharing your observations with other adults can help to build up a clearer picture of individual children and to identify any movement problems. Observing children in physical play and seeing how they respond to equipment and activities, including those they tend to avoid, can provide valuable insights. Seeing how children relate to each other and their coping strategies in different situations will all help to inform further planning and provision.

Climbing equipment

Objective

To develop co-ordination skills through whole body actions.

What you need

Fixed or portable climbing equipment with different escape routes (if possible). A-frames to which planks, ladders and slides are attached at various levels. Impact absorbing surfaces can reduce, but not prevent, injuries when falling from a height greater than 60 centimetres.

What to do

Where possible, choose equipment which can be arranged in different ways. It can be set up for a particular stage of development, so different groups of children are more likely to be drawn to it. It can also be arranged for more imaginative play, for example, as a ship. Set out a range of equipment with contrasting levels of demand, for example, a challenging arrangement of climbing, hanging and swinging equipment contrasted with a lower A-frame with low platforms and easy exit points.

Always consider the range of options open for children to get down, once they are up. For example, hanging and dropping or jumping from platforms. Over a period of time try to vary the arrangement of the equipment so as to avoid one group dominating it each time.

What to look for

Position yourself so the activity is in your view. Most children will move within their own limits of confidence and ability. Remind them that there is 'no touching each other' when on the equipment, and stand in a position where you can keep checking this. A limit on numbers using the equipment may well be needed. Praise sensible, safe climbing.

Look to see how individual children handle the problems set by the layout. When climbing, encourage a firm grip with fingers over and thumb under each rung. Initially, one limb moves and three are fixed. More confident climbers will move a hand and a foot at the same time. Getting down is often less predictable, so check that safe space is available for dropping, sliding or jumping.

Equipment for arm supporting activities

Objective

To use and strengthen trunk and arm muscles and to experience being upside down.

What you need

Arch climber, horizontal poles, planks, ropes, ladders.

What to do

Supporting body weight on arms helps the children use their upper body muscles, and as they bring their knees up they use their abdominal muscles too. Fixed poles at different heights are ideal for children to hang onto with their hands, keeping their feet off the ground, then swinging their legs or dropping back onto their feet.

Poles fixed at a lower level also encourage children to hang over and roll around them. Ladders and poles at a higher level can be used by children to hang from their knees or move along supported by hands, backs of knees or heels. Seeing the world from upside down is a useful orientation activity for general body awareness and later on, gymnastic skills. All equipment needs to be positioned so landings are safe.

What to look for

Children enjoy the sensation of hanging from their arms with their feet trailing. Look for a firm, supporting grip with hands positioned slightly apart. If children hang from their knees, check that there is sufficient space underneath for their back and head to move freely. Ensure that children dismount carefully, landing on their feet each time.

Balancing activities

Objective

To help children improve their balance, at ground level, on slopes and raised surfaces, in stillness and in action.

What you need

A selection of A-frames, planks, balance bars, fixed sections of tree stumps, tyres set in the ground or as stepping stones, lines on the ground, ropes.

What to do

Set up equipment with different balancing challenges. In the early stages, very narrow surfaces at floor level, like a line, can encourage walking and hopping. By arranging planks or beams raised slightly off the ground, or a series of tyres at ground level, children will practise dynamic balancing as they walk along, or static balancing as they try to keep still. To balance on a wide platform will be quite demanding for some children if it is raised well off the ground.

Slopes provide children with a different balancing experience, and increasing the height or narrowing the balancing surfaces gives further practice for more confident and agile children. Combining balancing with other actions, like climbing or jumping, helps to improve co-ordination as the children change actions as they move.

What to look for

Balancing requires concentration, general co-ordination skills and muscular strength. Notice the degree of concentration and care needed by individual children as they position their feet or hands to keep their body balanced. Look to see whether any children need you to stand by and offer a hand to them for the first cautious step. Focus on general encouragement rather than real physical support. See which children move in a well-balanced way with fluency and control. Try to provide increased challenges for the more competent.

Wheeled toys

Objective

To encourage co-operative skills and develop muscular strength by pushing and pulling each other on wheeled toys.

What you need

A selection of wheelbarrows, push-me pull-me toys, platform trolleys, trailers, caterpillars on wheels, buggies, materials for loading, containers.

What to do

Wheeled toys provide important equipment for role play. In a confined area you may need to restrict their use to one part of the play space. The focus should be on children working together, so choose toys which can be linked or allow at least two children to play with them, and have the further potential for transformation into adult forms of transport (like a 'pretend' fire engine or a lorry). Children can push and pull each other around or work together, as on the caterpillar.

If crates or boxes are placed in or near to trailers, children can practise packing, pulling them along, emptying and stacking them. Muscular strength is needed for moving material or other children, particularly if slopes are involved. Encourage children to make roads, add ramps, roundabouts and parking areas to improve steering and control.

What to look for

Check that certain children do not dominate the activity all the time, and intervene if this happens. Look and listen to see how they play alongside and co-operate with each other. Watch for safety when children are playing on slopes. See how they alternate between pushing, pulling or holding on as they discover at first hand about forces and momentum.

Trikes and bikes

Objective

To develop control in steering and manoeuvering a wheeled toy.

What you need

A selection of bikes and trikes.

What to do

These toys can dominate a space, generate aggression and be the sole focus of activity for some children. However, they do provide others with a vital opportunity to practise their balancing, pedalling and steering skills in a safe space. Choose when and where the bikes and trikes are made available. By riding them along lines, or a narrow pathway which include curves and turns, children can improve their steering and practise speed control.

What to look for

Check that all the children who want to use them get a turn. Discourage excessive speed leading to lack of control. Look for a good sense of balance and encourage careful co-ordination of body and wheeled toy.

Using balls and other games equipment

Objective

To provide opportunities for exploring the properties of balls and games equipment, and improving hand/eye/foot co-ordination.

What you need

Various balls, quoits, bean bags, ropes.

What to do

Children need opportunities to play with balls and other small equipment at an early stage. Gradually, they begin to predict how balls react in different situations and important co-ordination skills are practised. As ball play can easily interfere with any other activity going on, it is often best to have certain times when only balls are available. Balls need to be 'user friendly', clean, and in good condition. Provide a variety of sizes as large ones will encourage kicking, two-handed bouncing, throwing and catching, while small ones encourage rolling and one-handed throwing.

What to look for

Balls must be kept within the play area and the children must watch, follow and pick up their own ball each time. Some children may choose just to walk around holding it before they are confident enough to drop, throw or kick it. Look out for individuals who show confidence with a ball and help them to practise more specific actions — bounce and catch, roll, chase and pick up, throw in the air, drop and catch. As children are trying out a particular action, check that the ball they are using is suitable in size and texture.

Markings on the ground or wall

Objective

To use a range of markings on the ground or wall for practising different skills and games with other children.

What you need

Permanent markings, blocks of coloured playground chalk for temporary markings.

What to do

A few permanent markings should help to stimulate activity; too many can inhibit it. Keep them simple, so they can be used for more than one activity. Running, hopping, skipping, jumping and balancing can be encouraged by marking footprints in trails or by varying the distances between them. Lines can be jumped over or ridden between. Very small circles can be used as stepping stones; larger ones for bouncing balls in and even larger ones can encourage circle games like 'Here we go round the mulberry bush' and 'The farmer's in his den'. Markings on the ground or on a wall can make interesting targets. Some examples of possible markings can be found on photocopiable page 95.

Temporary markings with coloured playground chalk can give a particular focus to an activity, like steering or parking practice, with children getting involved in the design. They also serve more immediate needs and can be modified or removed later on.

What to look for

Are the present markings positioned safely in relation to any fixed equipment? If not, discourage their use and try to remove them. Note how the children use any current markings. Can other equipment, like a few bean bags, be placed near targets to stimulate activity? Do the children need some ideas? Are there activities that the children are already doing which could benefit by having some temporary or more permanent markings made?

Activity circuit

Objective

To introduce children to orientation activities by planning and following set routes around equipment.

What you need

A selection of cones, skittles, canes, hoops, low climbing equipment, tunnels, balance bars.

What to do

Choose equipment which will encourage different actions and pathways, for instance: balancing along, jumping over, scrambling through, going in and out. Arrange the equipment to make an interesting circuit so children have to change their spatial orientation as they go around it. Use as much space as possible so pathways between pieces can become set features; children can jog backwards around them or jump from one hoop to another. Show the children the layout and ask them to go around it in a set way, for example clockwise, but tell them they can begin at different points on the circuit. When they are familiar with the layout, encourage them to have set starting and finishing points to their route and to plan their own movements along the route which they can repeat.

A development from this would be to separate out the types of equipment and to place a red or a blue cone by each piece. Ask the children to make a route around the 'red' or 'blue' equipment by using only those pieces marked by that coloured cone.

What to look for

Check that the equipment is securely positioned and all the children can cope with the arrangement. Look to see that there are no obvious bottlenecks and likely collision points. See if the children keep to a set route and can describe their pathway using appropriate language.

Follow up

For older groups this type of activity can be linked to simple map-making activities involving symbols, plans and patterns.

Progression in physical activities – catching

Chapter three

Progression is vitally important when developing physical skills. This chapter provides examples of progression which focuses on the skill of catching.

Activities need to be well-planned, capturing the children's initial interest and encouraging them to practise. Repetition of actions is vital when establishing safe, effective movement patterns, but young children often need help in modifying their actions as they practise. Progression will be limited if children merely repeat actions which are inefficient or sometimes unsafe.

All physical activities make some demands on a child. Identifying some of the key features in an activity which are necessary for success will help in planning a suitable 'match'. Individual children can then be helped to achieve success in the activity and meet new challenges with enthusiasm.

Improving the control of actions

As children play, practise and become more skilful, they gradually adapt the way in which they perform their actions. They get the sequence right when skipping with a rope, the timing gets better when they catch a bouncing ball and they use the right amount of energy to jump over obstacles. Unnecessary parts of the movement are eliminated and actions are performed with less effort, more control and with greater accuracy.

Once a safe, secure pattern has been established, children need to meet and respond to new challenges as well as to repeat familiar movements. New challenges should stimulate the children's interest, making them want to get involved. Children like to feel that actions will be fun to do and that success is likely. Progress comes from wanting to practise, putting the necessary effort into the task, and giving it their full attention.

Extending the range of actions

Most actions can be performed in a variety of ways once a relatively consistent movement pattern has been established. In some actions, like balancing, different parts of the body can

act as the base for support and can also be the focus for variation. In others, like rolling, children can move in different directions, either stretching out or curling up. Some actions, like running, can be done at different speeds. The size of the action can change, as in jumping striding or hopping. Some actions can be practised on the spot or on the move, like bouncing and catching a ball, and more than one action can be linked together.

By giving children a rich variety of activities, their repertoire of movements can be increased. They are then more able to select the appropriate movements when they meet new situations. This variety should help children move more safely, adapting their movements where necessary and becoming more confident and imaginative movers.

Catching

This is a basic action which all children need to develop, and school may provide the only opportunity for some of them to practise this important skill. When a child throws a ball, she is releasing a ball she is already holding, but in a catch she has to predict the flight of a moving ball and get to the right place at the right time before the catch can be made successfully. A successful pattern of catching needs a lot of individual practice with large, light balls in the early stages. Later on, it is important to practise catching smaller balls which are thrown in more varied ways. Each of the following ideas provides a new challenge for children and should help them to enjoy their increasing ability to control and secure a moving ball.

Send and chase

Objective

To follow the movement of a ball and collect it before it stops.

What you need

Large, soft, light balls, brightly coloured and made of foam, plastic or pvc-coated foam.

What to do

This works best outside with a small group in an empty space. Let the children choose a ball and feel its size and texture. Ask them to try walking/running around the space keeping the ball firmly in their hands. Show them how to send it with a low underarm or sideways throw so it stays close to the ground. Get them to watch it, follow it and collect it. Can they catch it before it stops moving? See if they can run past the ball, turn to face it and collect it.

What to look for

Do the children send the ball with the right amount of force so they can catch it up? Do they watch the ball all the time from it leaving their hands to collecting it? Hands should reach towards the ball and gather it safely into the chest each time.

Sticky fingers

Objective

To improve visual tracking of a bouncing ball and hand/eye co-ordination.

What you need

A range of light, bouncy, colourful balls and a firm surface.

What to do

This can be done with a small group in an outdoor play area or with a larger group in a hall. Ask the children to choose a ball and hold it in front of them, hands 'sticking' to it. Ask them to push it down so it bounces on the ground in front of them. Tell them to watch the ball bounce up and down and see if they can stick their fingers back on to it. Expect a range of responses, from a first time catch to complete misses.

What to look for

See if the children push the ball down to the ground hard enough to make it bounce. Are their eyes on the ball all the time? Do they turn their head away? See when and where they place their hands to try and catch it. They need to put them under the ball as it drops down from the top of its bounce.

Follow up

Can the children push down harder so the ball bounces more times? Can they count the number of bounces before they catch it? Try using different balls. Which are easy and which are difficult to play with?

Up, drop and catch

Objective

To develop a straight upward throw, to follow the path of the ball and to improve the timing of the catch.

What you need

Balls of different sizes which bounce.

What to do

Ask the children to collect a ball that they think they can catch and to hold it in front of them with both hands. Ask them to throw it gently upwards so it bounces in front of their feet. Tell them to watch it carefully and get their hands ready to catch it after one bounce. Can they throw it higher and still catch it after one bounce?

What to look for

The throw should go straight up so the ball can be seen all the time. See if the children use the right amount of force in the throw, and release the ball at the right time to do this. Their hands need to move under the ball as it comes down from its bounce. If it seems too easy or too difficult, encourage the children to try doing it with a different type of ball.

Follow up

Develop the idea so the children are throwing the ball forwards as well as upwards and having to predict where it will drop more carefully.

Safe as houses

Objective

To practise and reinforce a successful catching pattern.

What you need

Balls of different sizes and weights, bean bags.

What to do

Ask the children to select a ball or a bean bag which they think they can catch easily. Tell them to throw it upwards and reach out with both hands to meet it. Their fingers and hands should close onto it and bring it quietly and safely into their tummy. Encourage them to change the ball if it keeps dropping. Ask them to count and see how many throws they can catch before one drops. See if they can make the throw a bit harder, a little higher, slightly more forward, still making a safe, quiet catch every time.

What to look for

Good concentration should be evident all the time. Look for a controlled upwards throw, eyes following the ball, hands moving upwards in line with its flight, then closing round it and bringing it down into the body smoothly. Hands should be facing upwards, little fingers nearer to each other than thumbs, when they catch the ball.

Follow up

See if the children can be successful using a smaller ball or bean bag, starting with short throws upwards. How many good catches can they do if they have one or two 'lives', losing one every time the ball is dropped?

On the move

Objective

To practise catching a ball which is moving away.

What you need

A range of balls, bean bags.

What to do

Ask the children to choose a ball they can catch safely. Ask them to toss it upwards so it lands in front of them. Can they catch the ball after one bounce? See if they can throw it forwards and catch it before it bounces. They will need to judge how far up and how far forwards they can send it so they have time to get their hands under the ball to make the catch. Some may find it easier to use a bean bag.

What to look for

Children should release the ball carefully so they have time to move into position. Look to see how well they are judging where they need to be and if they are balanced or moving when they make the catch. If they get into position but keep dropping the ball, get them to try a smaller throw. Encourage a safe catch every time with the ball or bean bag safely against the body. Children who achieve this easily should try a smaller ball or throw it further forwards.

Follow up

Encourage the children to count safe catches, trying to beat their own score. The activity can be made harder to do by throwing the ball further ahead.

The wall game

Objective

To practise catching a ball which bounces back off a wall.

What you need

A range of balls which bounce, a high wall.

What to do

Have just a few children try this unless there is a long wall. Ask them to choose a bouncy ball and throw it at the wall from about three metres away. Let them try different ways of throwing the ball so it comes back for them to catch. Most children will find it easier if the ball bounces before they catch it. Some will be able to direct the force more carefully and react more quickly, catching the ball before it hits the floor. Can they find different ways they can send it and still catch it?

What to look for

The children should stand far enough back, allowing plenty of time to respond to the ball's rebound off the wall. Check that they send it high enough. They need to move in line with the ball as it comes towards them with hands and fingers pointing forwards rather than upwards. Look for a quiet, smooth action with the ball brought safely into the body.

Follow up

Get the children to try a smaller ball, running forwards to catch it early. They could also play with a partner, one sending and the other catching.

Help a friend

Objective

To catch a ball travelling towards them from a partner's co-operative throw.

What you need

Bean bags, light balls of different sizes.

What to do

In pairs, the children should choose a ball. Show them how to help a friend catch it by standing one to two metres away and sending a gentle underarm throw towards their partner's tummy. The catcher's hands and fingers should reach towards the ball and close around it, bringing it carefully in. How many catches can they help their partner to do? Suggest they take a step backwards or try with a different ball to make it harder.

What to look for

Check that the children really are trying to help their partner by sending a careful throw. Catching a partner's throw needs good skills of predicting the pathway and time of arrival of the ball. If any turn their head away, or even close their eyes as the ball comes, suggest they use a softer ball. If some find it difficult, ask them to try catching from a partner's bounce or even collecting a rolling ball.

Follow up

Get the children to count their successful catches. Some can decide a target score before they begin. The thrower could try sending the ball a little higher, lower or to the side, so the catcher has to move her hands quickly to get them in line with the ball.

My catch game

Objective

To extend catching skills by experimenting with new ways to throw and catch, and to 'make a game'.

What you need

Balls of different sizes and textures.

What to do

Ask the children to collect a ball and practise their throwing and catching. Can they make the catch harder, for example, by adding claps, throwing the ball under a leg, trying to catch it in one hand or turning around before catching? Get them to try out different ideas, then plan and practise at least two ways which they can make into a game. Suggest that they share a few ideas to stimulate further variety. This idea could be repeated several times before the children make a game which works well. Let them describe and show their ideas.

What to look for

Children should experiment with some new actions and not rely solely on tried and tested ones. Initially, there will be plenty of dropped balls as they test themselves. Many will modify their own actions through practice, varying the force of the throw and predicting where they need to place their hands.

This experimental stage is important, but try to ensure that their trial and error does lead to success which can be reinforced.

Follow up

In pairs, see if the children can observe and copy each other's games. Try a game of numbers — for example, throw, clap and catch three times, then throw, bounce and catch three times.

Name that catch

Objective

To combine listening skills with a quick movement response to get into a safe catching position.

What you need

A large ball, preferably soft. Marked circles on a play area are useful.

What to do

Organise the children into groups of four to six. Ask each group to form a circle with one child standing in the centre with the ball. She throws it high and, as she releases it, calls one of the other children's names very clearly. She then runs out to join the rest around the circle. The child whose name was called runs in and tries to catch the ball either before it touches the floor or after it bounces. Then she repeats the idea.

What to look for

The throw should be straight and high so that the child has plenty of time to respond and move into position. In the early stages, it is best if the child faces the one whose name she will call so that the latter hears clearly. Eyes should be on the ball as each child moves in, hands and fingers pointing upwards, pulling the ball safely into her body. Check that all the children get a turn.

Follow up

The activity can be made more challenging by increasing the size of the circle or by encouraging the thrower to make it harder for the others to guess who should catch by not looking at the catcher before they call.

Moving into games

Chapter four

Children love playing games. Their enthusiasm for any activity can be captured easily if it is called a 'game'. They enjoy playing games with other children, like 'tig', with simple rules and little or no equipment. The challenge and excitement of chasing and dodging each other is matched equally by their desire to control balls using hands, feet, sticks and bats.

Children need plenty of opportunity, time and encouragement to play freely with different types of equipment, later on learning more specific skills as they control the equipment better. In the early stages they play on their own, later on sharing ideas and activities with others.

The equipment

There needs to be a good range of different types of equipment available for children to use. Balls are available in foam, foam and plastic coated, and plastic, measuring from six up to 20 centimetres. Some balls bounce high, some bounce low, some will be rugby shaped, but all need to be 'user friendly'. Children need to have a choice of types available to match different levels of competence. Ideally there should be enough balls of each size for them to have one each.

Small, lightweight hockey sticks and rackets/bats with large hitting surfaces help children to practise early dribbling, hitting and batting skills. Bean bags, quoits, hoops, skittles, long and short ropes, cones and canes give children opportunities to develop a range of actions in their own individual way.

Organise the equipment so children have easy access to it and can collect and return it to its proper storage space. Four baskets of equipment, one in each corner of the play space, usually work well for most activities.

40

Activities and skills

Skills young children need to practise on their own

Possession skills with ball or bean bag
- walk and carry, then run;
- drop and collect, then catch;
- throw upwards, watch it drop then catch;
- bounce and catch;
- roll along floor with hands;
- dribble along floor with feet;
- dribble along floor with a stick;
- pat into air with bat;
- bounce onto floor with bat.

The content of the games session

In the early stages children need a balance between individual play with equipment, and group games with no equipment. Later on they may be able to handle some equipment with a partner or in a small group. Energetic, running-type games with simple rules help to raise children's heart rates and should form a part of each games session.

Sending and collecting skills with bean bags, balls, bats and sticks
• roll, chase and collect;
• throw sideways, underarm, overarm, chase and collect;
• kick, chase and collect;
• strike with bat/stick, chase and collect;
• send against wall and collect;
• aim at, into or between targets.

Skills which should be practised with a partner or in a small group

• roll and collect;
• bounce and catch;
• underarm, sideways throw and catch;
• kick and trap;
• strike with bat/stick, catch or return
• young children should be encouraged to practise skipping with a rope, first individually, then alongside others.

The teacher's role

Children need much time to play with games equipment, gradually increasing their control over it and practising many different actions. If a child is having some difficulty, encourage her to change the equipment or the action. For example, she may be trying to skip with a rope which is much too long, so show her how to wind it round her hands. She may be dropping a catch because she does not gather it into her body safely. Children enjoy making up games on their own and should be encouraged to do so.

41

Treacle

Objective

To improve control in running and stopping.

What you need

A good sized space.

What to do

Check that the children know that treacle is sticky. Ask them to run on the spot and on the signal 'treacle' they must stop, with their feet sticking to the floor. Give them a clear signal to run again. When they understand the rules, let them run around, slowly at first, then more quickly, reminding them to listen carefully for 'treacle'. Vary the length of time between each 'treacle' and encourage the children to run faster as they become more confident.

What to look for

Look for a smooth, well-balanced action which the children can stop easily with one foot in front of the other, and their arms out helping them to balance. Their arms should swing rhythmically from the elbow as they run and their feet should not slap the ground too noisily. The children need to look around as they run, avoiding others and trying to keep their action smooth.

Follow up

The activity can be made harder by running in a smaller area. The children need to avoid others as they run and try to keep a well-balanced action.

My ball

Objective

To improve co-ordination by watching and handling moving balls.

What you need

Sponge and plastic balls of different sizes, and baskets, a good-sized safe space, preferably outdoors.

What to do

Organise some baskets in the space, each one containing the same type of ball. Show the children the different types of ball and name them — for example, plastic, sponge, big, middle-sized, small — and show them where they are kept. Send the balls across the space and ask the children to go and collect one and bring it back to the right basket. Repeat and ask them to bring the same (or different) type back. Then let them choose a ball to play with on their own. Ask them to find a space and to play sensibly.

What to look for

Look to see which children are happy to send the ball away and follow it, and which choose to keep it very close to them. Check that the children who send the ball away follow it with their eyes and then move after it. As the children play with the balls, name the actions, for example, kicking, bouncing or throwing. Ask them what they like doing best with the balls. What is easy? What is hard?

Follow up

Can the children choose a ball and tell you what they are going to do with it? Encourage them to use their hands and their feet to move the ball.

What's this?

Objective

To explore and discover some ways of handling unfamiliar equipment.

What you need

Some familiar equipment in baskets (for example balls and ropes), a basket of some unfamiliar equipment (for example, quoits, bats or hockey sticks).

What to do

Arrange the baskets around the edges of the playing space. Show the children the unfamiliar equipment and name it. Make them aware of what other equipment there is to play with and remind them about playing sensibly. Let them choose their own equipment.

What to look for

Notice which children choose familiar equipment and which try something new. Check that they are playing safely, for example, the hockey sticks should be kept near the floor and not swung high into the air. If necessary, suggest one or two ideas for them to try. Show a few new ideas to the others in the group, naming them and describing how the children performed them.

Follow up

Introduce other different pieces of equipment along with familiar ones so children are encouraged to become involved in a wide range of activities.

Let's all skip

Objective

To improve the co-ordination of hands and feet in a skipping action (jump rope).

What you need

Ropes, seven and eight feet long.

What to do

Ask the children to collect a rope each and place it on the floor in a line. Get them to jump forwards and backwards over it smoothly. If they can do this easily with a good rhythm, suggest they pick up the rope and hold it behind them, one end in each hand, with the rope just touching the floor when their arms are outstretched. See if they can swing the rope over their heads and when it hits the floor jump over it, 'slap, jump'. Encourage them to repeat the action without stopping. Ask them to count how many times they can do it.

What to look for

When the children jump over the rope on the ground, look for a smooth, rhythmic action. When they begin to skip, check that the rope swings over and touches the floor just before the jump is made. Some children may find it easier to run over, rather than jump over, the rope.

Follow up

Ask the children to try different ways of skipping, for example, running, hopping, or going backwards. Do they know any rhymes for long rope skipping? For example; 'Salt, pepper, vinegar, mustard' (begin slow and increase speed).
   'Raspberry, strawberry, applejam tart, Tell me the name of your sweetheart . . . ABC . . .' (keep going until the jumper trips).

Soccer stars

Objective

To improve foot control when dribbling a ball.

What you need

Medium balls, (soft kick footballs are ideal), a good-sized space.

44

What to do

Ask the children to choose a ball and dribble it around the floor with their feet, trying to keep it near them all the time. Encourage them to tap the ball using the side of the foot, mainly the instep. At times they will need to stop by putting their foot on top of the ball, and looking around before moving into another space.

What to look for

Some children will tap the ball so gently it hardly moves, some will kick it too hard. Look to see which part of the foot they use and if they swing their foot against the ball with a small action. See if they are well balanced, with their body weight over the ball and not behind it. The more skilful children will look up as they dribble and be able to stop the ball without having to look at it all the time.

Follow up

See if the children can dribble the ball and stop it on a signal. Can they go a bit faster and still stop it easily? If there is plenty of space, ask them to practise giving the ball a short kick, running after it and giving it another kick.

Hit that ball

Objective

To develop the skill of hitting a stationary ball along the ground with a bat or a hockey stick.

What you need

Short-handled, light hockey sticks, cricket bats or round-shaped bats; light, small and medium balls, plastic pucks.

What to do

The children need to have had some opportunities to become familiar with the equipment. Ask them to collect a ball and send it along the ground with their hand so it goes flat and straight, then to run after it. Then get them to collect a bat or stick and bat the ball along, chasing after it.

What to look for

Check that the ball is stationary before the children try to hit it. Look to see that they stand sideways on, holding the bat so the flat surface is behind the ball. Hockey sticks can be held either way round if they are flat on both sides; play the ball so the hand at the top of the stick is across the body. The children should be well balanced and touch the ball with the bat or stick first, swinging back and then forwards to hit the ball.

Follow up

See if the children can hit at targets or between imaginary goalposts for accuracy. If they are using a bat, suggest that they drop the ball on the ground and then try to hit it.

Hoop bounce

Objective

To improve control and accuracy in ball bouncing.

What you need

Hoops of approximately 92 and 61 centimetres (36 and 24 inch) diameter and different-sized balls.

What to do

Ask the children to choose a ball that they think they can bounce and catch well, then find a space and practise. Then ask them to collect a hoop, place it on the floor, and see if they can bounce their ball inside the hoop. Can they pat-bounce their ball inside the hoop? If they are successful, suggest that they walk or run to another hoop and repeat the activity. For example, they could go to hoops which are the same colour as their own hoop or go to hoops which are a different colour from theirs.

What to look for

Check that all children have a ball they can use successfully. Look to see if they push the ball down to the floor in a straight line with enough force so they can catch it. The more skilful children should be able to do a few pat-bounces, pushing the ball down at the top of the bounce. As they move around, look to see that the children hold the ball directly above the hoop before they bounce it.

Follow up

See if the children can find other ways of bouncing the ball with the hoop, like moving around the hoop while bouncing

the ball in the middle or standing in the hoop and bouncing the ball around the outside.

Are you ready?

Objective

To improve accuracy in throwing a ball or bean bag for a partner to catch.

What you need

Selection of large and medium balls, bean bags.

What to do

Show the activity to the children and explain it. The ball is thrown backwards and forwards between the two players. It helps if the thrower says 'are you ready?', before the ball is sent, using a one- or two-handed underarm throw. The catcher should stand about two metres away with her arms and hands showing

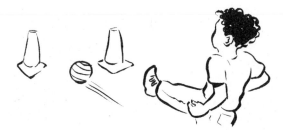

where she wants the ball. Ask the children to find a partner and to choose a ball which they can both catch. After a few successful catches, ask the catcher to 'show' the hands higher, lower or to the side and see if the thrower can still throw accurately into them.

What to look for

Check that the hands of the catcher are asking for the ball each time and that the thrower sends a well-directed throw with the right amount of force. Look at the children's feet: they should be well balanced, usually with one foot in front of the other slightly apart as they throw and catch the ball.

Follow up

To make the activity more difficult suggest that the children stand a little further apart or see if the thrower can throw the ball slightly away from the catcher's hands each time.

Score a goal

Objective

To plan and set up an activity to improve accuracy in rolling and kicking a ball.

What you need

Medium and small balls, soft kick footballs, cones or markers.

What to do

Ask the children to get into pairs. Set up a goal mid-way between two players and explain the activity to them, showing them how to be careful when they roll or kick a ball to their partner, so that they 'score a goal'. One of each pair collects a ball and the other collects two markers. Get them to find a space, arrange their markers to make a goal and decide how far away from their goal they will stand. See how accurate they can be when rolling or kicking the ball through the goal. If they are finding it too easy or too hard, ask them how they can change it.

What to look for

Look to see how the children have planned their activity and if they roll or kick with a carefully co-ordinated and well-directed action. See if they line up with the goal and look at it before they swing their arm forwards, to roll the ball smoothly. If they are kicking, check that they stand sideways and kick the ball with their instep. Look for a careful preparation and follow-through on each action.

Follow up

Get the children to work out a way of making the activity more difficult. For example, see if they can score three or four goals in a row, make the goal smaller, or stand further away from the goal.

Stations

Objective

To give further practice in a range of games activities and to learn to bounce a ball on a racket.

What you need

Four types of equipment. For example: 1. skipping ropes for free play; 2. small rackets and small, light balls; 3. hoops, quoits and bean bags for aiming; 4. big balls and cones for foot dribbling.

What to do

Organise the children into four groups so they can move around the four activities. Choose a variety of activities, for example, one new one, two familiar ones and a free play one. Focus on the children using bats or rackets with balls. Ask them to see if they can place the ball on the racket face and keep it there, then try to walk around with the ball balanced on the racket. Let them try to make the ball bounce up and down. The children may need to hold the racket with both hands to get better control over the bouncing action. After a few minutes stop them and rotate the groups so everyone gets a turn with each piece of equipment.

What to look for

Look to see if the children watch the ball all the time. They need to grip the racket handle firmly as this will help to keep the hitting surface flat. Although the main focus is on one group, keep an eye on the other groups and when you stop them, let one or two children from each show their ideas to everyone before they move on to a new activity.

Follow up

See if the children can give themselves a target, for example, three bounces or more before the ball falls onto the floor. Suggest that they try to send the ball higher or bounce the ball with the racket held in one hand.

Ball practice station

Moving into gymnastics — floorwork

Chapter five

Few activities are more exhilarating to children than those which test their sense of adventure, skill, strength and balance. For example, climbing on to obstacles and jumping off them, hanging upside down, swinging, sliding, rolling, and balancing in precarious positions are natural activities that most children perform if they get the opportunity.

These activities all involve a degree of physical risk. Learning to assess risk and move with control, safety and confidence are essential skills young children need to develop. They require regular, well-structured opportunities to practise a wide range of movements, learning to trust their bodies and try out new ideas. Activities leading to gymnastics, both at floor level and on apparatus, practised in a secure environment, help to develop this trust. These activities are also important in helping children develop strong, flexible and agile bodies through supporting their weight in different ways.

Body actions

With young children, the focus is on improving the quality and extending the range of actions which they already do quite naturally, rather than on teaching them a series of prescribed skills.

Travelling
This involves shifting the body weight from one part to another as the body moves. This can be done using only the feet, using hands and feet, rolling over on to other body surfaces or sliding, pushing and pulling the body along. Travelling on higher apparatus will involve climbing, hanging and swinging along with the arms taking the weight.

Balancing
As children travel, they will have moments when they lose momentum and almost balance in stillness before moving off again, often at speed. Finding different bases to support the body weight, such as shoulders and knees and moving into and out of balances slowly, are useful activities for developing general movement control. It is important from an early age to practise actions which share and later support the weight of the body on the hands.

Jumping and landing
Leaving the ground and coming down again is exciting but quite a difficult action for young children to perform well. With practice they discover how to control the timing and the force of the jump so they can get higher into the air and land without falling over.

Improving control and sensitivity

Well-controlled movement is almost always safe movement. All actions have a natural rhythm and children should be encouraged to improve the natural timing of their own actions. The actions may have a clear start, middle and finish, like a single jump, or they may consist of the repetition of a single movement as in climbing. In each case, sensitive movement control is needed as the child's body stretches high in a jump, landing softly, or climbs in a well-balanced and carefully co-ordinated action.

Extending the range of movements

Children need opportunities for practising natural body actions in ways which are different and even unconventional. They should be encouraged to try moving in different directions, to vary the shape of the body as they travel, jump, turn and balance. By varying the speed and energy of each action, children increase and enjoy the range of movements their body can do.

Sequencing movements

Children love the flow of movement and get caught up in continuous action, often finding it quite difficult to stop. Sometimes different movements are linked quite naturally as a child climbs, twists, hangs, swings and then jumps down. Sometimes similar movements are repeated, like running and leaping around a space. Changing from one action to another with control requires agility and sensitivity. Children can be helped to link together similar or differing ideas which have a clear starting point and a steady

finish. The following ideas can all be practised in a good sized space and on a floor surface which is clean and not slippery. Mats will not usually be needed.

Ready for action

Objective

To gain attention and focus on copying simple movements as a warm-up activity.

What to do

Begin with the children sitting or standing near you. Ask them to watch you carefully and to copy what you do. For example, raise both hands and stretch them high, lower them and touch the floor lightly. Vary this by shaking one hand then the other, both together, low or high. See if the children can move their head, their shoulders, shake their feet, make circles with their hands, touch their head with one hand, their tummy with the other. Gradually change the speed and size of the movements to see if they are all still watching you and copying.

What to look for

The focus is on gaining and holding the children's attention, and helping them to concentrate on using specific parts of their body as a warm-up activity. Watch them closely, and after giving them an idea that they must copy, try not to say anything. Observe which children find it difficult to perform simple movements or to keep in time with you.

Follow up

It can be useful to have one of the children acting as leader, and showing movements very clearly for the others to copy.

What to do

The children begin near you. Ask them to walk quietly away from you and sit down in their own special space. Let them practise an activity in that space, like jumping up and down, stretching up high or balancing. Then touch some of them lightly and ask them to walk/run in and out of those sitting on the floor. See if they can remember their own space and sit down in it again. Repeat with other children. Gradually have more children on the move, concentrating on moving in and out of all the spaces. When all children are familiar with finding their own special space, ask them to move around using different actions, for example hop, stride, bounce.

What to look for

Check that all the children have a safe space on their own in which to do their movements. When they move around, look to see that they move in and out of each other without touching anyone and if any have difficulties knowing who they were sitting near to, give appropriate help.

Follow up

Find new safe places to sit or stand after finishing each activity.

Special spaces

Objective

To develop an awareness of finding, moving from and returning to a safe space.

52

Bouncy feet

Objective

To improve co-ordination and resilience in jumping and landing with feet together.

What to do

Ask the children to find a safe space, then to bounce up and down on the spot, like a bouncing ball, keeping their feet close together. See how quiet they can be and then let them practise bouncing around the spaces. There will be variations in the length and height of the bounces, but they should try to keep the action smooth, not jerky. Let them practise a contrasting action to this one, such as big, slow strides into big spaces.

What to look for

As the children bounce on the spot, look to see whether they bend their hips, knees and ankles as they go down, then stretch out as they go up. Encourage them to bend at their knees as they touch the floor lightly. Look to see how they use their arms; some will move them up and down as they bounce, helping them to spring lightly and to keep well balanced.

Follow up

To extend this activity, the children can do opposites, for example a few big bounces reaching forwards, then a few small nearly on the spot; or a few close to the floor, then a few high into the air.

Sharing the work

Objective

To explore ways of moving with hands and feet in order to share body weight.

What to do

The children should be in a space on their own ready to begin. Ask them to put their hands and their feet on the floor and to 'walk' their hands around their feet, trying to keep the latter still. Then let them move around the space with hands and feet sharing the work. Some will move one hand/foot before the other and some will move both hands/feet. Some will face the floor, others will face the ceiling and some will alternate as they go. Some children will move very quickly and others very slowly. Let them try different ways of using their hands and feet.

What to look for

As the children move, they should have the palms of their hands on the floor with their arms strong and straight. Look to see that their arms are taking some of the weight, and not just touching the floor

occasionally. See how quietly and carefully they place their feet as well as their hands on the floor each time. Describe the actions you see the children doing and show a few examples, focusing on the different ways they are moving.

Follow up

To develop the activity, the children can try opposites, for example, moving quickly then slowly or going forwards then backwards.

Quiet rolls

Objective

To practise rolling over sideways, quietly and safely.

What to do

Check that the floor is clean and safe. Ask the children to stretch on tiptoes with their fingers high, arms by their ears. See if they can make the same shape on the floor, lying on their back. Ask the children to roll over onto their tummy very slowly and then to keep on rolling over. When they get near someone else, they should roll the other way. Ask them to curl up in a small ball, either on their back or facing the floor, and tip over quietly and roll sideways.

What to look for

Children should move quietly and carefully, making the action safe. Look

for a clear body shape. When they stretch out to roll, they should keep their body firm and straight, each part slowly touching the floor as they move. In a tucked roll, check that the action is smooth with knees and elbows tucked in. Show examples of quiet, careful actions.

Follow up

To develop quiet rolling further, see if the children can link the two ways together or roll slightly faster, still moving quietly.

Take a photograph

Objective

To improve control when moving into and holding a balance.

What to do

Ask the children to move quietly on their feet or hands and feet. On a given signal, like 'photo', they should stop and touch the floor with a different part of their body, for example two hands and one foot, or their bottom, stretch out slowly, then keep very still. When ready, 'take a photograph', by saying 'click' or using a crisp sound, then ask them to move around again. See if the children can find different bases for support, like shoulders, knees, one hip, or try two, three or four parts touching the floor. Encourage them to hold each balanced position for a few seconds only, trying not to wobble.

What to look for

Look to see that the children support their body firmly before they stretch out into a balance. Show a good example of a slow, careful balance and let the children identify which parts are touching the floor. Help them to see how they can stay balanced by making their muscles work hard to keep still.

Follow up

To develop this idea, see if the children can link together two or three different balances, making two or three different 'photographs'.

Feet high

Objective

To practise supporting body weight on hands in a safe and controlled way.

What to do

This idea follows actions involving hands and feet sharing body weight. Ask the children to put both hands on the floor, shoulder width apart, and to bounce their feet up together behind them, getting their bottoms high. Their feet should come down very quietly. At first let the children practise on the same spot, but later encourage children to put their hands down in different places. This helps them to vary the amount of force they need to push their feet up, as well as developing their sense of balance and orientation.

What to look for

Look to see that the action has a clear start and finish. Check that the children keep their arms straight and strong with their head looking slightly forwards. See if their arms are vertical from the floor so they have a good chance of bouncing their feet up high. If some children push their feet up too hard they need help in landing safely. Suggest that they move a hand forward to bring the feet down properly. Show safe, controlled examples of the action, describing the key features.

Follow up

Suggest that the children try swinging one leg up before the other to get their feet up higher, then landing safely as above.

Patterns

Objective

To make and improve a pattern of two different actions linked together.

What to do

Ask the children to practise a favourite action, for example a pattern of skips, jumps or hops around the spaces. The movements should have a clear start, be well controlled and have a tidy ending. Then let the children try a different way of moving — for example, rolling over or using hands and feet and repeating the action several times to make a pattern. Let them choose one way to begin with, practise it a few times, and when you say 'change it' practise the other action a few times. See if they can keep the change very smooth, so making a pattern with two different actions in it.

What to look for

Being well balanced and ready for the first movement is important. Look to see whether the children can finish their last action carefully after a 'finish' signal. As they practise joining different actions together, see how well the end of one action merges into the start of the next one. Use a good example of a smooth link to show the group.

Follow up

This idea can be used for many actions, both similar and different. Children can also choose their own patterns, for example, one of sideways movements.

Action replay

Objective

To develop a movement memory by practising and repeating a simple pattern of movements for a partner to copy.

What to do

Choose an action as the basis of the pattern, like jumps or travelling on hands and feet. Ask the children to work out a pattern of easy actions that they can repeat accurately, like four different jumps or two forwards and two sideways actions using hands and feet. Let them practise to get the action right so it has the same rhythm every time. Ask the children to find a partner and sit down. One shows her pattern while the other watches and then the two try to do it together. Remind them to be safe and to try any new movement very carefully. When it works well, change over and let the other child show his pattern.

What to look for

Check to see if there are any pairs in which the abilities are very different. See if any actions need to be modified for this particular activity. Look to see that children have a clear start and finish and are repeating their movements so they are the same each time. Keep the pattern short. Restrict the number of movements if they seem to be different each time the children practise them.

Follow up

A natural progression would be for children to work out a pattern together, either matching movements or creating a mixture of matching and mirroring movements.

Moving into gymnastics – using apparatus

Chapter six

Using apparatus is greatly enjoyed by young children as they test their increasing agility, strength and confidence. Regular opportunities to practise skills like climbing and jumping from various heights are important in helping them to handle their body weight safely. Apparatus arrangements should provide variety in levels and widths of surfaces, textures, heights and angles of slope.

Young children develop an understanding of size and shape as they handle their body successfully through three-dimensional space. Using apparatus also provides much valuable exercise for all muscle groups, particularly the upper body and arms.

apparatus is arranged. This can be:
● individually, such as hoops, mats, benches, climbing frame;
● with a few pieces together, like an inclined plank, a low table and a mat;
● in 'stations'; each arrangement providing different experiences (high or low, jumping or balancing, climbing or rolling).

Safety

Apparatus needs constant checking for signs of wear and tear. Surfaces should be kept clean and hygienic. Any problems should be reported and any apparatus that is damaged must be removed from use until it is properly repaired.

Apparatus should be stored for easy access, with heavier items positioned around the edges of the space, so that any handling is done over a short distance. Other equipment, such as the piano and television/video, should be positioned so as to cause as few safety problems as possible.

Planning and positioning apparatus

The actions produced by children are largely dependent on the way the

Young children need to practise lifting, carrying, placing and replacing apparatus safely, but it is important that they have plenty of time to use it as well. In the early stages they should have some opportunity to collect their own apparatus, like a hoop, and place and use it in a safe space. This can be extended to two children carrying a mat or a balance beam. They should carry equipment over the least possible distance with guidance given on careful lifting.

Children also need opportunities to use a wide variety of apparatus, such as low tables, planks, benches, mats, tunnels and a climbing frame. This usually means positioning most of the apparatus before the session, thus allowing plenty of time for activity. Queues tend to form in a linear arrangement if there is only one obvious starting and finishing point, so try to include a few options in the layout. Keeping the same layout for several sessions will help the children become familiar and confident in using it. Gradually, they can be allowed to carry and position most of the apparatus for themselves, handling the same pieces for several sessions.

Using the apparatus

Rules about using the apparatus need to be made clear, and understood and accepted by all the children. They include:
- one child on one piece of apparatus at a time
- working very quietly
- no touching or pushing
- getting down carefully and sitting away from all the apparatus on the teacher's signal.

In the early stages, the children should be encouraged to explore the apparatus freely. Later on, grouping the children is valuable — letting them work at one station for a few minutes then moving on.

Role of the teacher

In the early stages the focus will be on children using the apparatus safely. Reinforce safe responses and intervene if a child's safety appears to be at risk. Observe the group from the outside, looking inwards; this helps keep the full group in view. Be careful not to distract children as they move; comment to them *after* they have completed a movement. Identify the action and comment on how it was done, for example: 'I like the way you really sank into the mat to land quietly and safely'. Once children are familiar with the apparatus, more focused

tasks can be given to extend the range of ideas and increase the quality of movements. In almost all cases these tasks will be sufficiently open-ended for each child to choose her own successful response.

Around the hoop

Objective

To place a hoop in a space and to find ways of moving around and in and out of it.

What you need

A hoop, 46 or 61 centimetres (18 or 24 inch), for each child.

What to do

Place the hoops in the corners of the room. Ask the children to collect a hoop which is near them and to place it in a space. See if they can move around it without touching it, both on the inside and the outside. See how many ways they can go around it on their feet, for example, running, hopping, skipping or 'running' on hands and feet. Let them try putting their feet inside and their hands outside the hoop and vice-versa. See whether the children can jump into and out of their hoop, using hands as well as feet to support their weight.

What to look for

Check that the hoops are well spread out. Look to see that the children are really concentrating on keeping close to the hoop. Look for well-balanced actions as they move in a small circle. Encourage them to move in alternate directions. See how the size of their actions matches the size of the hoop. Identify and describe their actions and show interesting ideas.

Follow up

To extend the variety of actions, support the hoop horizontally upon two skittles and have the children working in pairs.

Naming actions

Objective

To name and practise different actions on mats and benches.

What you need

Mats and benches, placed around the edges of the room, one piece for three or four children.

What to do

Organise the children to carry and position a mat or a bench carefully. Ask them to sit down by their piece of apparatus, but not on it. Let them explore moving along and over the benches and mats, using the 'one at a time' rule. Encourage the children to move with different parts of their body touching the apparatus, for example, sliding along a bench on their tummy. Invite them to find different ways to move along and over the bench or mat. Then change the groups around so they can use a different piece of apparatus.

What to look for

Look to see that the children take turns safely. Children will delight in repeating actions which they enjoy. Describe their action, let them repeat it, then suggest that they try something else. Show different ideas and let the children

suggest names for them.

Follow up

Encourage the children to decide upon and name their actions before they set off, so helping them have a more careful plan to follow.

Don't touch yet

Objective

To increase spatial awareness by moving in and out of the spaces created by the apparatus.

What you need

Low tables, mats, planks, tunnel, benches, soft play shapes.

What to do

Set up the apparatus so that it is well spread out, with plenty of gaps and holes. Ask the children to find a space on the floor, not on a mat. See if they can walk carefully around the room, going in and out of the apparatus without touching it or each other. Encourage them to go under some pieces, through gaps, or over pieces but still without touching. They will be making judgments about size and shape as they move. Then let them get onto and off apparatus quietly with hands or feet touching.

What to look for

Check that there are different pathways that children can take as they move. Look to see that they move carefully and safely until they are familiar with the layout. Describe the pathways that the children take – over, under, around, in and out – and show some interesting examples.

Action stations

Objective

To practise actions which involve supporting body weight on different parts.

What you need

A climbing frame, two trestles linked by a ladder, plank or pole, mats, benches and balance beam, different heights of tables.

What to do

Plan and set up the apparatus to encourage specific actions at each station, for example: a climbing, a jumping, a balancing and a rolling station. Ask the children to find a place to begin and to move carefully, keeping to the 'one at a time' rule on each individual piece. The children can work on pieces of their own choice, but once familiarity is gained let them work in groups of five or six, spending a few minutes on each set of apparatus before moving on.

What to look for

Stand in a position where you can observe all the children and see that they are working safely and quietly. Check that the climbers on the frame are gripping firmly at three points as they move a hand or a foot. Climbers on the ropes should always have enough energy to come back down hand over hand, never sliding. See whether any children seem anxious when they are above floor level or on a narrow surface. Children who are rolling over backwards should try to place their hands on the mat by their ears to help them push over. Those going forwards should have their hands on the mat and tip over slowly with their chin on their chest.

Going on a journey

Objective

To practise safe actions along, over and under a variety of apparatus.

What you need

Benches, planks, tables, hoops, mats, climbing/arm supporting apparatus, tunnels, soft play shapes.

What to do

Arrange the apparatus in 'stations' so that low pathways are created around about it. Include some inclines, different levels and a choice of entry and exit points. The children can be grouped and help to position some of it. Ask them to find a safe place to start at their 'station' then move on the apparatus carefully. Encourage them to use different parts of their body as they move. Suggest that they try to 'go on a journey' from one piece of apparatus, across the floor to the next piece. Urge them to make their journey as interesting as possible, for example: walking, using hands and feet, jumping, rolling over and pulling through.

What to look for

See that children are getting onto and off the apparatus carefully and concentrating as they move. Describe their actions and the path they take, encouraging a change of action when they move onto a new piece.

Follow up

This idea can be extended by encouraging variations, like going sideways or trying two different actions on the same piece of apparatus.

Safe landings

Objective

To improve resilience and control when getting off apparatus from different heights.

What you need

Low tables, inclined planks, benches, mats.

What to do

The children can help in setting up the apparatus by placing mats by the tables. There should be a choice of heights from which they can jump and land. Remind them about careful 'squashy' landings and ask them to find a place to start. Encourage them to bounce along the benches using feet or hands and feet and to land quietly on both feet. When they are confident and showing good resilience, see if they can jump upwards a little way from the apparatus, still landing carefully.

What to look for

Before children get down from a table or other surface they need to see that there is a safe place to land, then try and look forwards. Look for bending at hips, knees and ankles as they bounce and land and using their arms for balance. Some will land and topple forwards, some will end up on their seats; see that they are steady and balanced *before* they jump.

Follow up

Extend this activity by asking the children to use their hands to support their weight either on the bench or the table and to bounce their feet onto, off or over the apparatus.

Something different

Objective

To extend children's range of actions by practising some new ways of using the apparatus.

What you need

A range of apparatus such as climbing frames, tables, planks, benches, mats.

What to do

Arrange the apparatus into stations, each group having two or three different pieces. Organise the children into groups, so they can work on each station for several minutes, practising some different ideas. Encourage them to try different ideas and see if they can tell you what they are going to try next time. Identify the actions like rolling, sliding, pushing and pulling and the direction of travel, speed or the shape of the body as it moves.

What to look for

Check that the children are trying out actions which are basically safe. Try and watch individual children have two turns and comment on the different ideas they are trying. This is a good opportunity to show a range of children's ideas so others can observe and try new ones in their own way.

Follow up

Once the children have tried different ideas, they can try opposites, for example: stretching to move along, then tucking up small.

Find a balance

Objective

To improve balancing skills during action and in stillness on raised surfaces.

What you need

Climbing apparatus, tables, wooden and padded planks, benches, balance beam.

What to do

Plan an apparatus arrangement which includes some natural opportunities for balancing using some individual pieces like a balance beam and an inverted bench, as well as inclines, raised planks and tables. Organise the children into groups and ask them to find places on their apparatus where they can stop safely and show a good balance. They should be able to balance with different parts of their body touching the apparatus for support.

What to look for

When children are on narrow surfaces, either inclined or slightly raised, some will find walking a challenging balancing activity. Some will be able to stop and hold a true balance using various points, like hands, knees, feet. Some will be able to balance with their feet high, for example, hanging from their knees on a climbing frame or in a shoulder or headstand on a raised surface. Children should be encouraged to try out more adventurous balances at floor level before using them on a raised or narrow surface.

Follow up

A development of this activity could be to see if each child can hold a balance on each piece of apparatus, before moving on again smoothly.

Do it again

Objective

To develop movement memory by repeating a series of planned actions accurately.

What you need

A range of different types of apparatus.

What to do

Plan the apparatus so that the children can use a station which includes at least three different pieces. Pupils can help in carrying and placing much of this, and they should be familiar with the layout. Encourage them to use all the pieces at their station and find ways of getting from one piece to another so their movements fit together. Look for a child who is doing this quite clearly, show it to the group and focus on the smooth links. Children appreciate repeating enjoyable movements so encourage this, helping them to start and finish actions with control. Give them plenty of time to improve their movement accuracy.

What to look for

Look to see that the children find their own way to use the apparatus, not merely copying the child in front. Some children will be able to complete one action and begin the next one without a pause; others will have less control and will need to regain their balance before setting off again. Show a range of ideas which display an improvement in accuracy.

Follow up

This activity might be developed further by asking the children to plan actions which are performed on the floor as well as on the apparatus.

Moving into dance

Chapter seven

All children can, and do, dance. From being babies, they have used movement as a way of expressing their feelings and have delighted in repeating rhythmical actions. When children are fully involved in movement for its own sake and in enjoying the sensations it provides, their movement takes on a quality which appears, and is, excitingly different from their everyday actions. The look on children's faces as they dance (alone or not) is evidence enough of their involvement and the significance of their experience. Their instinctive desire to dance must be valued and nurtured, with regular opportunities provided for them to respond to a range of stimuli, both spontaneously and under guidance. As their range of movements increases, children gain great satisfaction from selecting, practising and repeating patterns of movement which express their ideas with increasing control.

Making dances

Right from the start, children should be involved in making dances. Creative work thrives when children are given a stimulus which captures their imagination and excites them into action. They need to express their ideas in an atmosphere where their efforts are recognised and valued. The stimulus for the dance might be a rhyme or a familiar story line, like 'The elephant and the mouse'; it might be a rhythm created by percussion (for instance, by a tambourine); or it might be words based on a topic such as the weather, like frost and icicles.

Planning action phrases to extend the children's range of dance movements is the starting point for the teacher. However, it is the children's movement responses themselves that are the real basis for further inspiration and development. Initially the dance may only have two contrasting types of movement, such as energetic skipping followed by a gentle turning action; later on it may have several sections which can be repeated with increasing accuracy.

Body actions

Ideas for dances need to be translated into body actions. All actions are based on travelling, jumping, turning, stopping or gesturing.

The development of quality and sensitivity in children's movement depends on their opportunities to experience, enjoy and practise a rich variety of these actions. As they focus on the different ways they can perform actions, children's movement comes alive, and it is this quality which is the essence of dance and must be fostered. Look at the following examples.

Travelling
This can be done by creeping, darting, striding, tiptoeing, running, marching, skipping or crawling.

Jumping
This can be done by leaping, bouncing, shooting, exploding, flying, hopping or soaring.

Turning
This can be done by spinning, spiralling, rolling, twisting, whirling, circling, floating or curling.

Stopping
This can be done by resting, balancing, freezing, crumpling, collapsing, falling, wobbling or gripping.

Gesturing
This can be done by stretching, rising, reaching, punching, collecting, sinking, throwing or touching.

Young children enjoy the sensation of the whole body being involved in actions, but some actions will focus more naturally on an individual part, like sharp elbows and knees when freezing in spiky shapes.

Contrasts

Help children to increase their range of movements by giving them contrasting experiences which make them more sensitive, confident and expressive movers.

In speed and strength

Actions like punching, freezing and gripping need firm, tense muscles, whereas actions like stroking and floating need light and delicate muscle control. When muscular tension is removed, the body feels floppy and gives in to gravity. Young children find quick actions exciting and exhilarating; for example, darting, exploding and changing body shape suddenly. To counter this provide opportunities for slow balancing or curling up movements and to enable them to feel the calming effect that slow motion movements can give.

In size and body shape

Young children can vary the size of actions quite easily — big strides, little steps, tiny jumps, huge leaps; exaggeration helps develop quality. Being absolutely still helps children to be aware of their body shape and how much space it takes up. Moving into and out of long, thin shapes, giant, wide shapes, small, ball shapes or spiky, twisted shapes in different ways requires concentration. All parts of the body play their part as a shape emerges, is held, or changes.

In spatial patterns

Exploring actions which contrast in direction, level and pathway as well as changing size and shape quite literally give movements a new dimension. As children sit or stand they can make

patterns by moving their fingers, hands or arms in all the space around them. They can go high and low, stretch out to the sides, go behind and in front making curves, circles, spirals, straight lines and zigzags. Other parts of their bodies, like elbows, can also make patterns, and as they move around children can make more patterns on the floor with their feet, going forwards, backwards and sideways.

Rhythms and phrases

All actions have their own inbuilt rhythms, from staccato hops to a smooth, floating turn; from an exploding jump to long, slow strides. Either by repeating the same action, like turning round and round with arms outstretched, or making a phrase of different actions, like running, leaping and falling, young children get caught up in the flow of the action.

Give children plenty of time to recognise and enjoy their own rhythms, plus time to practise improving the natural way one action flows into the next. Give them opportunities to practise some actions which do have a more regular rhythm as well, like wheels turning or balls bouncing. Encourage their movement memory by patterning actions into phrases, such as: jump and jump and jump and freeze — each phrase showing a clear starting and finishing position. Gradually children will be able to repeat phrases with greater control and expression.

Accompaniment

The teacher's voice is so important. *How* words are communicated as well as *what* is said helps to establish a more creative atmosphere and to hold the children's attention as they dance. Words can give a signal for starting and for finishing a phrase of movement. The more descriptive the language, the easier it is for children to develop quality and sensitivity in their movements.

Using percussion instruments increases the range of accompanying sounds, as well as providing valuable signposts within and between movement phrases. It is relatively easy to play these in different ways, at times as a stimulus to dance and at times to accompany what the children are actually doing.

Pieces of recorded music (on tape) which have a clear focus, like a lively rhythm, a pleasing melody or a particular atmosphere, are invaluable in stimulating a qualitative movement response. The music should enhance movement and not overpower it. Many tapes of short pieces prepared specifically for children's dance are available. The children need time to become familiar with the music before they can benefit fully when moving to it.

Inside the nursery

Encourage children to enjoy using their bodies with confidence and improve movement co-ordination in as many different ways as possible. Opportunities for listening to music and using a sound table in the nursery can be extended if a small space can be created. A listening and dancing activity can be set using well-known action rhymes, or children can respond spontaneously to music which is playing quietly. Most of the following ideas are more suitable for a larger space.

My hands can . . . my feet can . . .

Objective

To develop awareness and control of different parts of the body in action.

What you need

A selection of percussion instruments, like a wood block, a tambourine, shakers, a triangle.

What to do

The first part of this idea is useful at the start of a session. Ask the children to come and sit by you. Tap quietly on the floor with your finger tips and ask them to join in. See if they can tap on the floor, then clap their hands together. In this way they are making a simple pattern of two contrasting actions/sounds. By adding percussion sounds, like tapping on a tambourine, the quality of the movements can be improved and clear signposts can be given for changing from one action to the next. Make a pattern of sound which is easy for them to repeat, for example, four beats with the accent on the last one.

Ask the children to stand in a space and do one action with one body part and one with another. For example, run on tiptoes then stretch hands up high and wiggle their fingers. It is useful to have two actions with contrasting qualities such as quick and slow or strong and light.

What to look for

Encourage the children to concentrate on the part of the body they are using to make their chosen action, such as wiggle, shake or stamp, so that the action is very clear. The quality of movements will be helped by your choice of instruments and the way you say words like 's-t-r-e-t-c-h'.

Follow up

Choose a piece of percussion and ask the children to show you a 'foot dance' or a 'hand dance' using the sound to help their body to dance.

Familiar rhymes

Objective

To increase movement confidence and control by matching patterns of movements to well-known rhymes.

What you need

A rhyme (or rhymes) with which the children are familiar, such as 'Incy wincy spider', 'Hickory dickory dock', 'Wee Willie Winkie', 'The grand old Duke of York', 'We're going on a bear hunt', 'Here we go round the mulberry bush', 'The wheels on the bus'.

What to do

Familiar rhymes are a valuable and enjoyable source of dance material. They provide rhythms which children find satisfying, as well as ideas which can be translated into actions easily. The children can chant the rhyme as they move, or you can say the rhyme emphasising certain words to help the actions become more expressive.

What to look for

Encourage children's own ideas and help them to exaggerate the quality of each action, like using their whole body to stretch out, running with very tiny, quiet steps or keeping very still in a curled up shape. Repetition is important in improving the flow and quality of movement patterns.

Follow me

Objective

To improve control in matching foot patterns to sounds which have a regular beat and rhythm.

What you need

A drum or a tambourine.

What to do

Lead the children quietly into the space and set off walking around the outside of the room beating the drum firmly, with the children following you. Most children will get 'caught up' in the tempo created by the beat and match their action closely, but some won't; it doesn't matter at this stage. Look around as you go and use your voice to help develop the appropriate quality, like 'l-o-n-g strides'. Give them plenty of time to move at one speed before you change it. It helps if you make the change very distinct, such as shaking the tambourine very lightly for quiet tiptoeing, or striking it slowly for long, slow strides. Try beating the tambourine in a more rhythmic way to encourage other actions, like skipping. 'Pop goes the weasel' is useful for this.

What to look for

Look at the expression on the children's faces as they perform different actions. This tells you if their whole body is involved; encourage this. There should be some variation in the size of movement and the amount of energy used in contrasting actions.

Follow up

A progression would be for the children to move in one long line or to add arm actions. Soon they will want to take turns at being the leader of the line or to dance alongside a friend.

Special shoes

Objective

To encourage children to perform basic body actions in a more sensitive and imaginative way.

What you need

A selection of percussion instruments or recorded music for contrasting sounds: strong, light, fast, slow, rhythmical, lyrical.

What to do

Play some quiet, melodic music or a pattern of sound on percussion such as chime bars or bells. Talk quietly with the children using words like gentle, smooth and calm to describe the sounds. Suggest that if they put on 'special dancing shoes' they can do special movements to this sound.

Ask the children to put on their 'quiet' shoes which will help them to do very gentle actions and to walk, skip or tiptoe around the room, keeping their whole bodies very light. When the sound stops they must stop moving but try and stay as light as possible. Let them try moving their arms and hands up high and down low or to turn around with the same feeling of lightness. Have alternate patterns of moving around and being on the same spot. Contrast this with 'strong shoes' which make their bodies firm and energetic so they can jump around the spaces, stopping and holding strong body shapes.

What to look for

Encourage involvement and concentration on the quality of the sounds you use. Look to see how carefully the children place their feet on the floor for gentle actions and if they can keep that degree of lightness right through their bodies. Contrast is important, so focus on helping them to *feel* the differences in muscular tension between the strong and light movements.

Follow up

This idea can be extended by wearing other special items, like a crown or a spacesuit, and exaggerating the quality of the actions which match them.

Balloons

Objective

To observe the qualities of a balloon when it is inflated, moves and is deflated, expressing these qualities in movement.

What you need

Balloons, a pump, a cymbal or a tambourine.

What to do

Careful observation of the movement of living things and objects can provide rich ideas for dance. It is the particular qualities which need to be identified, rather than attempts to reproduce an action as the children see it. Blow up a balloon very slowly and let them see how it changes shape. Get them to show you how they can grow into a particular shape very slowly. Encourage them to balance, not only on their feet, but also on different parts of their bodies. If you use a sound, include clear starts and stops. Show them how quietly the balloon can go high and come down to bounce along the floor without a sound.

Let the children practise jumping on the spot or in different directions, each time landing with an exaggerated, quiet, bouncy action. Ask them what would happen if there was a gentle breeze. Let them show you how gently they could set off, rise up, sink down or roll over. See if they can add some twists and turns as they move. Let them try to move like different shaped balloons.

Finally, the balloon can burst quickly or lose all its air slowly. Practise energetic explosive jumping and collapsing to the floor, matched to a firm beat on the tambourine, or moving quickly with jumping, turning, whirling movements which get smaller as the balloon deflates.

What to look for

Help the children to move into interesting shapes. Look for sensitivity in the quality of quietness and lightness of the whole body as it changes shape and keeps in balance. A delicate touch is needed when different parts of the body contact the floor after jumping or rolling over. See if the children can maintain their 'balloon' shape as they move around. A real contrast should be seen between the gentle drifting and the more energetic ending.

Ready . . . go . . . a-n-d stop!

Objective

To improve co-ordination by practising a pattern of movements which fit together, showing a clear start and finish.

What you need

A selection of percussion instruments, like a tambourine, a large cymbal, shakers.

What to do

Ask the children to find a space quietly and to sit still and listen. Play a pattern of sound, for example, beat a tambourine to a familiar rhythm like 'Humpty Dumpty' and then stop. Suggest an action which would fit the sound, like making a pattern of jumps around the space.

Let the children find a starting position and, when everyone is ready, play the pattern of sound and let the children practise. Ask them to show you their starting position each time before you begin playing, and tell them that they should start to move only when they hear the sound. When the sound stops, their movement should stop too. Play the same pattern each time so they get to know how long their actions have to last.

Repetition will help the children to focus on the flow of their movements. Repeat the idea using different instruments, such as beating a cymbal then letting the sound die away for a gentle turning action down to the floor, or a drum beat for strong punching action with the arms.

What to look for

Look for starting positions which clearly involve all the body, like arms outstretched ready to turn. When the sound ends, the body shape should not collapse but be held clearly as suggested by the sound. Show and describe examples of clear starts and finishes.

Freezing and melting

Objective

To use movement to express children's observations of running and frozen water.

What you need

A woodblock, a tambourine, a cymbal, hard and soft beaters.

What to do

'Weather' is an excellent starting point for dance as it can be linked with children's direct observation and other classroom experiences. It helps if children have seen and felt the firmness of ice and its clear shape. Ask them to balance in a strong, icicle shape with elbows and hands playing an important part. Play sharp sounds on the woodblock so the children can keep changing shape using their whole body. Shake the tambourine gently and suggest that one part of their body is getting warmer and is going to melt, like a hand which gradually flops down, then each part in turn, or the whole body can slowly melt down into a 'puddle'. A cymbal, beaten softly, helps the 'melting' movement.

Contrast this with a pattern of light, sustained movements to suggest running water. For example, travelling lightly and adding a turning movement with hands going from low to high with a shaking tambourine as accompaniment. By adding beats on the tambourine, see if the children can gradually make their movements stronger until they stop on one strong, loud beat, in a 'frozen' shape.

What to look for

Emphasise the importance of the whole body being strong or light or relaxed and floppy. Focus on the muscular tension individual children show, and demonstrate examples which *look and feel* right. Encourage the careful transitions between the frozen and running water once the extremes have been practised.

Follow up

This dance can be developed into a partner dance where pairs of children can work out their actions together. They can also take it in turns to be the leader to freeze then melt each other with alternate strong and lighter stretching and twisting movements.

Opposites

Objective

To develop more quality and control in movement by performing some sudden actions and some slow and sustained actions.

What you need

Contrasting sounds from percussion or from recorded music.

What to do

The idea of opposites is a valuable one for young children as it helps them to experience how it feels to move with contrasting qualities.

Play a sound which has a very clear quality, like striking a woodblock sharply, and ask the children to move an arm or hand on each sound making a sharp, jerky action and then keep still. Each action should be done so fast you can hardly see it. Try asking the children to move other parts, for example, see if they can move both arms at the same time, or their arms and one knee. Have a gap between each strike so you can see their interesting shapes. Make a pattern of about six of these.

Contrast this with silence and ask the children to creep around with long, very slow steps, moving so carefully that you cannot hear their feet touch the floor. Combine the two ways of moving, focusing on the differences in speed, exaggerating as much as possible. The idea can easily be linked to other ideas, like the mouse and the elephant, or to video fast-forward or slow motion.

What to look for

The stimulus is very important, as is your voice, to create the atmosphere for each movement. Young children need much practice in developing more variation in their movements. Describe and praise individual responses, showing examples of real contrasts.

Drawing patterns

Objective

To practise drawing patterns in the air and on the floor imaginatively, and keeping well balanced.

What you need

A cymbal, a glockenspiel or recorded music.

What to do

Begin by asking the children to watch your hand as it 'draws' a smooth pattern in the space in front of you, with one, then the other hand. Ask them to show you a big pattern made in the air using their hands, based on curves, circles or straight lines. Always ask the children to show you their starting position. A sound accompaniment can help them to draw a pattern and provides clear signposts for starting and finishing the phrase.

Contrast this with a pattern on the floor, like running lightly in and out of each other, or drawing big circles on the floor by skipping. Children can combine the two patterns together by having a clear 'change' signal on percussion, or let them choose their own actions for their 'pattern dance'.

What to look for

Remind the children to look at their hand as it moves, and to keep changing hands. Encourage them to reach up higher, down lower, out to the sides further and round behind them. Look to see that they are involving the whole body as their actions become bigger, and that they are keeping well balanced. Show interesting examples to inspire more imaginative patterns. Some children will begin to lead the action with other surfaces, like the side of their hand, or their elbow; encourage this sensitivity.

Follow up

Ask the children to draw patterns of circles, spirals, zigzags, letters, numbers and so on, using contrasts of size and speed.

Dance a conversation

Objective

To take turns with a partner to make clear phrases of movement matched to clear patterns of sound.

What you need

Recorded music with clearly defined phrases, or a percussion instrument.

What to do

With the children all together, play the music and ask the children to join you in clapping along with it. Then clap for one phrase only, listening quietly during the next one. Repeat this so children get the feel of when phrases start and finish without needing to count out loud. Ask them to find a partner and to stand near each other in a space. Then play the music so they can practise a pattern of actions — for example, skipping and keeping near to their partner, stopping in a clear shape at the end; or making slow twisting and turning movements, then balancing in a strong shape. Make sure the phrase is long enough for them to get into the movements before they have to stop! You will probably need to tell them when to start and when to stop each phrase at first.

Follow this by having a number one and a number two in each pair. Illustrate the idea of a 'conversation' with one couple — number one moves and holds a shape, then number two does the same. This can be repeated so each moves at least twice. If they are quite close together they will find it easy to see when their partner has finished so they can start.

What to look for

Children need to be able to feel the phrasing in a piece of music. Many will do this easily, while some will only start and stop their movements by observing others and/or hearing your cue. See if the children look at their partner as they move. Encourage movements which seem to fit the shape made by their partner. Show a range of 'conversations' to help new ideas to develop.

Moving into athletics

Chapter eight

Running fast to 'tig' a friend or avoid being caught, and trying to jump further than last time, are familiar examples of activities which test children's natural desire to see 'how fast', 'how high' or 'how far' they can run, jump or throw. Children experience great pleasure from taking part in activities which use speed, strength, stamina and flexibility and where the thrill of the chase is usually sufficient motivation for all-out effort.

As children make up and play their own games, striving to improve on earlier efforts or beat a friend, they begin to accept and respond to simple competition in a positive and natural way. Learning to cope with success and sometimes failure is important, but the emphasis should always be on full and energetic involvement. Many activities which lead to athletics involve children competing against themselves so they develop skills of co-operation as they practise alongside others. They need to develop these basic motor skills all year round.

keep the focus on energetic and enjoyable involvement. Organise this sensitively and try to arrange for small groups of similar abilities to run together. Forty metres is the maximum distance recommended by the English Schools' Athletic Association that any child under seven should run at full speed, so adjust distances accordingly with regard for age and individual differences. Relays are based on taking turns; simple ones can be introduced early on with an emphasis on enjoyment. Gradually, more steady running can be practised as children learn to pace themselves.

Running

Most young children enjoy running fast, and this is done best in a safe, open space. Look to see if any child shows signs of undue stress when running fast over short distances and monitor them carefully. Some children will need specific help in developing an efficient running technique, but try to give them plenty of practice in these early stages. They usually run flat out for a short distance then have a brief rest, getting their breath back before setting off again. Chasing games, like 'tig', or 'tail chase', naturally involve this type of running and if the action can be combined with another one so much the better. Carrying objects, like bean bags, from one hoop to another helps to develop agility skills as they stop, reach down and change direction, as well as practising running.

Children do delight in testing themselves against others, but try and

Jumping

Natural actions of hopping, skipping, leaping and taking 'giant strides' are automatically practised as children jump and land, sometimes on one foot, sometimes on two. They discover that they can jump further if they run first and enjoy jumping across lines, and onto and off low obstacles. They need to find their 'best foot' for jumping and with a variety of skipping ropes, skittles, canes and hoops, as well as lines marked on the play area, they can find plenty of ways to test out these skills.

Combining running and jumping together improves spatial awareness as well as timing and co-ordination skills. A soft grassy area is preferable for activities where landings are likely to be unsteady.

Throwing

A safe space is essential for young children to practise throwing different types of balls and bean bags for distance and, at times, for accuracy. In the early stages they should experiment with different ways to throw a ball — underarm, sideways or overarm. Observe their pattern and help it to become more efficient. Older children should be taught the overarm throw which is the basis of many other skills. Throwing from a line, and collecting on a given signal, will be necessary with a larger group or in a more confined area — safety must always be the first consideration. Later on, children enjoy seeing how far they can throw and try to beat that distance. As is the case with jumping, working with a partner is helpful as the other person can mark the distance of the throw more accurately.

Organising the session

Many activities will naturally take place in games sessions; some running and jumping will be done in gymnastic sessions. If the focus is specifically on these skills, then a balance must be provided in the amount of stamina, strength and agility each activity demands.

Running activities are practised best with all the group together, so there are natural rests between bursts of activity, and the pace can be monitored more easily. Throwing for distance is safest when all the group is concentrating on one activity. Group work can be organised where jumping over lines and small obstacles is involved.

Going running

Objective

To improve co-ordination in the basic running action.

What you need

A big space with a non-slippery surface (outdoors on grass, if possible), cones, markers or bean bags spread out over the area.

What to do

Bring the group close to you and ask the children to run up and down on the spot, making their knees and arms work hard. Follow this by asking them to stand next to a marker. Ask them to run around the play area touching markers as they pass them.

Remind them to look where they are going and not to touch anyone else. When you give a signal 'stop' or 'freeze', the children must slow down, then keep very still. Give them a clear signal to start again. Let them have short bursts of running, followed by brief rests.

What to look for

Check that the children are using all the space, and trying to avoid others while running. Look for a well co-ordinated action, with arms swinging backwards and forwards from the elbow, and feet pushing the body forwards with good-length strides.

Show good examples, describing how the way they use their arms or lift up their knees helps them to run further. Give individuals positive and encouraging comments about their own action.

Follow-my-leader

Objective

To practise running at a steady pace to raise heart rate and work co-operatively to lead or follow a partner.

What you need

A good sized space.

What to do

Ask the children to find a partner. Choose one pair to help you show and explain the idea. Standing one behind the other, a good stride apart, the leader sets off running with the other child following and copying close behind. Show them how to turn and face the other way so the other child can become the leader.

Let them all have a go, then on a clear signal they should stop and turn, with the other child taking over as leader. Do this several times so children learn to adjust their running speed.

What to look for

Encourage the leader to run at a steady, even pace which is not too fast, and to look for spaces to run into. Remind them to swing their arms and to breathe all the time they are running. Look for real co-operation between pairs and show examples.

Follow up

The activity can be extended by asking the children to make patterns and pathways with their running action while always keeping to the basic forwards running action.

Racing

Objective

To practise starting on a signal and running fast in a stright line to a set point.

What you need

A flat, safe area at least 40 metres long, start line, bean bags/markers.

What to do

Fast running is best done on dry grass. Make clear paths for running by using two bean bags of the same colour for each child. Place one at the start and one at the finish, about 15-20 metres away. Arrange the bean bags at least 2 metres away from the next child's. Ask the children to find a partner and then to join with another pair to make a four. Each group lines up in turn, each child placing one foot up to and behind the start line or each child standing next to their marker. Show them how to lean forwards, pushing off hard and fast and punching with their arms as soon as they hear the start signal. Tell them what you will say, like 'get ready...go'. Ask them to run in a straight line to their own colour marker.

Remind them to run very fast right to the finish and then walk back to you along the side of the track. Arrange children in groups of similar speed once you are familiar with their abilities. Let each group have a few more turns each.

What to look for

Look for a good 'ready' position using the whole body. As the children run, look to see that their feet are pointing forwards, their arms are swinging backwards and forwards, and they are driving onwards with good long strides. Remind them to look in front and keep their head still. Watch for any child who veers off at an angle. Encourage an all-out effort and look for any child who seems stressed.

Follow up

Once children are running in small groups of similar abilities and are familiar with fast running right to the finish, some groups will enjoy being timed. Give individuals their times in seconds, calling out 6, 7, 8 and so on — as they finish.

Shuttle relays

Objective

To practise and enjoy fast running as a member of a small 'team' and to build up stamina.

What you need

As for 'Racing'.

What to do

This will work best if children have done a simple pair relay first, such as taking turns at running up to and around a marker, back down to a line and touching a partner's hand for them to go. Gather the children together and ask them to find a partner, then join up to make a four. Demonstrate the activity with one group. Position one pair at the start, one behind the other, with the other pair opposite them at the finish line. The first one at the start runs down the track carrying a bean bag which she hands over to the first runner from the other pair waiting at the finish line. This child runs back with it and hands it to the second runner at the start line and so on until all four runners have had a turn. Let them all have a go.

Focus on enjoyable participation, rather than competing group against group. All the children should have a go at being the first runner.

What to look for

Check that there are good gaps between each group for safety. Make sure the children understand how the race works and know who to run towards. It helps if the 'next' one stands with their hand up so that each runner knows who to give the bean bag to.

Look to see that the children swing their arms and run in a straight line, only holding out the bean bag as they slow down at the end.

Jump the river

Objective

To practise combining a run and a jump in a well-controlled pattern of action.

What you need

One skipping rope for each child.

What to do

This activity is safest on dry grass as landings may be unsteady. Let the children practise a run and a leap to see how far they can go, finding their 'jumping foot' and trying to land on both feet. Look for a well co-ordinated example to show the group. Ask each child to collect a rope and find a partner. Place two ropes on the ground about a metre apart, then show and explain the idea to them. Stand a short way back from the rope, run fast to take-off behind one rope, jump the 'river' and land over the second rope. Each pair then finds a space and decides how far apart to place their ropes. Give the children plenty of practice to get the combined action right, before they focus on jumping further.

What to look for

Check that each child has a short run-up. See if they can begin to plan their run-up, accelerating as they run, trying to get close to the first rope at take-off. Encourage them to jump upwards and reach forwards with their arms. Help the children to co-ordinate the action better and bring their take-off leg forwards to land with both feet together.

Broad jump

Objective

To develop leg strength, improve control and increase distance in a two-footed standing jump.

What you need

A marked line or a skipping rope, small markers.

What to do

This activity can be practised in most playing spaces. Ask the children to find a space and stand with their feet side by side and slightly apart. Let them practise seeing how far forwards they can go in one jump. Remind them to land on two feet each time and keep still. Ask the children to find a partner and use one pair to show the idea using the lines on the ground or a rope. One child stands with her toes to the line (or heels to the rope), and jumps. The child's partner

stands a short distance away and places a marker level with the back of the heel. They take turns at jumping and marking for each other, trying to jump past their own marker.

What to look for

Look for a well-balanced starting position with body leaning slightly forwards and knees bent. The children's arms should swing down and back, then forwards as their legs extend and push the body forwards. Check that they land firmly, bend their knees and keep their arms forwards to prevent them from falling backwards. Show a good example, pointing out these key features. Encourage them to observe carefully, so they can mark their partner's jump accurately.

Follow up

As children become more interested in beating their own best jump, they can begin to measure, either using non-standard measures like their own feet, or metre rules.

How high?

Objective

To practise jumping over a barrier at different heights.

What you need

Activity skittles, short canes.

What to do

This activity needs a firm surface. Ask the children to find a partner and collect two activity skittles and a cane, which they carry vertically for safety. Show them

how to place the cane on the skittle on the side 'away' from the jumper, so that it will fall off easily if knocked.

Suggest to the children that they start off with the cane very low and find ways to jump over it. They can move the cane higher as they become successful. Direct each pair to a specific space.

What to look for

Check that each pair are positioning their cane correctly. They only need to run a few steps before taking-off, so discourage long run-ups. The highest point of their jump should be directly over the cane, so notice where they place their foot on take-off. It needs to be at a suitable distance from the cane.

Look to see which children run straight forward and 'hurdle' over and which approach it at an angle. As the height increases, encourage the children to run from the side, so the leg which swings high first is nearer to and alongside the cane. Show a successful example of this.

Beat your throw

Objective

To practise throwing in a straight line, trying to beat their own 'best throw'.

What you need

Bean bags, a start line or long skipping rope.

What to do

Children must throw into safe spaces away from other children. Ask each child to collect two bean bags of the same colour; one for throwing and one for marking. Have a line or a long skipping rope as a start line. Show the activity to the children, throwing one bean bag in a straight line forward with an underarm action. Try to throw the second one even further. Run to collect the nearest one and bring it back to the start line, always leaving the further one as a marker. Remind the children to look before throwing, then to try and throw the bean bag in their hand further than the one out on the ground or the floor.

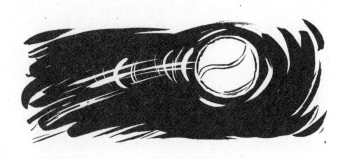

What to look for

Help the children to throw in a straight line with an underarm action by placing the opposite foot from their throwing arm forwards to the line. Their arm should swing backwards then forwards, releasing the bean bag from a straight arm. Some children will sling it sideways, across their body. Encourage them to stand sideways on so the bean bag goes forwards as they release it.

Follow up

Children can practise this in pairs, using a small ball. One can throw, the other can use a bean bag to mark where the ball touches the ground.

Overarm throw

Objective

To help develop an effective overarm throwing action.

What you need

Small balls, a start line or long skipping rope.

What to do

This is an important skill which children need help to develop. Make sure there is a big safe space to throw into. Ask the children to find a partner and number themselves one and two. Number ones should collect a small ball and spread themselves out along the start line with one foot forward. Number two should stand a few metres back. Show the children how to hold the ball well back with their elbow bent and ask them to throw it straight ahead, straightening their arm as they release it. On a signal from you, the children run after their ball, carry it back and give it to their partner. Let them have several turns at throwing as well as looking at some good examples.

What to look for

The opposite foot from the throwing arm should be forwards, with the body sideways on. Look for the elbow leading the action until the sudden flick of the wrist at the end helps straighten the arm. Show a throw which works well, encouraging the children to look at one key feature as they watch. Praise individual effort and reinforce effective patterns as they emerge.

Follow up

Overarm throwing can be done against targets on a wall, aiming for accuracy. Encourage children to make up their own game, by throwing from a certain point and deciding on a set number of turns.

84

PE across the curriculum

Chapter nine

Physical activities make significant contributions to children's all-round development, apart from their obvious importance in promoting physical development. Movement is the context in which much learning occurs, as children practise and develop a wide range of skills and experience and internalise many different concepts. As the whole body is involved, physical activity can act as a powerful agent for learning: feedback from the performance is immediate and the associated images and sensations are often long lasting.

Learning by means of the physical has much cross-curricular potential in the early years. Movement activities, however, must retain their integrity and have value in their own right. They must not be contrived merely to serve other curricular ends. Links which exist naturally need to be identified and made more explicit; in this way the integral nature of moving and learning can be exploited more fully.

Cross-curricular themes

Aesthetic educaiton

Aesthetic education is highlighted in movement activities as children practise and perform movements which are pleasing to the eye as well as satisfying to carry out. All physical activities can contribute to this, but gymnastics and dance have a particular role in helping children to observe, identify, appreciate and describe movements which have a pleasing line, shape, pattern or rhythm.

Health education

Physical activity has much to contribute to health education. Children are automatically interested in new life, growth and development and especially interested in their own bodies. Children learn how to keep their body safe and how to move safely; they learn about personal hygiene and about sensible eating and drinking. If children take part in a range of meaningful activities on a regular basis from an early age and gain a sense of achievement, they associate exercise with fun. The 'feel good' factor is crucial in establishing the exercise habit early on.

Health related fitness
For some children the school environment may provide them with their only opportunity for vigorous exercise. All body systems benefit from regular exercise, but the cardio-vascular and musculo-skeletal systems in particular need it for efficient functioning.

Having experienced faster breathing, an increased heart rate and the warm glow which comes from exhilarating and exciting activity, children will want to recapture the pleasurable sensations which energetic activity generates.

Stamina
The ability to keep on playing a game or chase a friend is improved with regular practice. Maintaining muscular activity and keeping a regular pattern of breathing without undue stress is easier when the body systems work more efficiently. Young children need energetic activity interspersed with periods of rest, as they have difficulty pacing themselves in the way older children can.

Strength
Making muscles work harder, often by repeating activities, helps to make muscles stronger. Many activities involve the whole body, but some use more specific muscle groups. Hopping and jumping improve leg strength, pulling and lifting improve trunk strength and climbing and supporting the body weight on arms improve arm and shoulder strength. Whole body actions will improve muscle tone generally, and children should be encouraged to stand and sit in a well-balanced and poised position.

Flexibility
Maintaining a good range of movement around the joints is important throughout life. Children should take part in activities, particularly gymnastics and dance, which involve extending the range of movements which naturally occur around each joint. Encourage them to stretch that bit further and to feel the difference when they do so.

Education for citizenship

Citizenship is a cross-curricular theme which permeates all education. Children regularly meet situations where their needs and desires have to be balanced against the needs of others. Issues such as individual responsibility and respecting the rights of others are often more evident during physical play activities as children share space, equipment and activities.

Cross-curricular skills

Practical skills

Physical skill development is a major focus of physical education, but practical skills are vital in many other areas of learning and deserve high status. Keyboard skills, writing, drawing, using tools, measuring, constructing and playing musical instruments all require movement control and precision. The more opportunity children have to practise and improve skills which use large muscle groups at an early age, then the more likely they are to perform fine motor skills with increasing accuracy.

Communication skills

Movement is a significant means of communication in its own right, and young children relish opportunities to express experiences, stories, ideas and feelings through dance and drama.

Listening to, understanding and following instructions are vital skills associated with all areas of learning, and especially so in movement activities, where individual and group safety are additional features. Children hear descriptions of movement from others, children and adults alike. They observe, recognise, name and describe movements for themselves as they talk with other children and adults. They can use language to plan and evaluate their own movement reponses and share their experiences and feelings with others. Encourage them to use the appropriate language for the activity while helping them to understand that when they *are* moving, they should concentrate on moving and not talking.

Problem solving

Children solve movement problems constantly throughout their play, and especially during physical activities. They respond to challenges and problems in their own way. Because the risk element is greater in some activities than in others, it is essential that movement problems can be solved in many ways to cater for the differing needs within the group.

Children need to understand the demands of the task and have the abilities and skills to solve it. Similar and previous experiences will be recalled, which makes earlier (successful or unsuccessful) movement experiences very significant. Sometimes the problem is set by the equipment, for example, travelling across a ladder supported by two A-frames off the ground. Sometimes the problem is set by the teacher, for example, working out how fast to roll a ball so that it can be chased and overtaken before it gets to a line several metres away. All children need to feel that success and satisfaction can be achieved, and so are well motivated when it comes to applying themselves fully to the task.

Working independently and alongside others

Physical activities are invaluable in helping children to become independent learners, as well as to co-operate sensitively with others. They learn to share space, equipment and often activities, and begin to understand how their actions affect others.

Subject links

In these early years physical activities can contribute to learning in other curricular subjects, often through a topic based approach, in these early years. It is important to identify where the natural links occur so other learning can be initiated, fostered or extended through physical activities. Some topic work has few obvious connections with Physical Education, and contrived links can sometimes discredit both the physical activity, the specific curriculum area, or the topic.

The following ideas suggest some ways that physical play and Physical Education help promote learning in other curricular areas.

English

● Children can listen attentively and follow instructions accurately, such as 'go to your colour corner, collect a ball and move it around the floor using your feet'.
● Place word/picture cards at each corner of the play space instead of giving verbal instructions for the task. For example, 'throw', 'bounce', 'kick', 'roll'.
● After observing a demonstration, encourage children to describe what they saw, for example, feet skipping gently, stretching out and pulling along slowly.
● Compare a pattern of movement with a sentence, each one having a clear start, middle and end.

Mathematics

- Children can count actions, like three hops, then three jumps or count the number of skips they can do with a rope.
- Ask the children to get into two's for a 'follow-my-leader' activity, with the child who is 'taller than..' standing in front of the other child.
- Children can place one quoit on the floor, take one stride away from it and throw two bean bags into the quoit. Then they could try throwing from two strides away, three strides away and so on.
- Play games which rely on making sets. For example, children run around, and on a given signal say 'two..three..or four' and they stand inside a hoop in sets of that number.

Science

- Ask children to point to, name and perform actions using different parts of the body, like foot, ankle, knee, elbow, wrist, shoulder.
- Play an energetic game and let children describe how they feel, like feeling warmer or breathing more deeply.
- Children will experience forces by pushing and pulling themselves along benches, up inclined planks and pushing off hard to get a fast start when running.
- Ask children to explore and describe properties and features of different types of balls, for example, which balls are best for bouncing.

Technology

- Help children to recognise the materials making their play equipment, and how the structure and the properties of those materials make equipment safe and strong enough for them to climb, swing, balance and jump on.
- Observe how things move. Through different actions children gain more awareness and appreciation of how their body moves at various joints. This can lead them to designing and making a simple product with moving parts, like a puppet.
- Provide crates, planks and construction blocks for role play so children can make sturdy, well-balanced structures for a particular function, such as fixing a plank on which to push up a wheelbarrow.

Geography

- Children can follow directions around the playground, like 'start behind the white line, run to the yellow line, then skip to the blue marker and come back to the white line'.
- Place four cards on the walls in the hall showing the compass points, North, East, South, West. The children can practise a pattern of turning jumps to face different directions. Make patterns of travel and turn using feet, and hands and feet.
- Observe and describe current weather. Help the children to translate words and ideas into action, like cold or hot; patterns in the snow; raindrops and running water.

Art

• Ask the children to record or represent a favourite play activity, or part of a Physical Education session, on paper using pencil, pastels, crayon, brushes and paint.
• After a Physical Education session children can use clay to make simple models of figures or shapes.
• Children can look at and feel objects with contrasting properties, shapes or textures, like smooth pebbles, sharp stones or a silk scarf. They can then express these qualities in movements, such as strong jagged shapes, gentle twisting and turning and so on.

Music

• Play 'musical statues' using recorded music which has a particular mood. Help children to capture the mood in movement, using for example quick, small movements or slow, large movements, interspersed with stillness when the music stops.
• Play recorded music with a rhythmic pulse and ask children to match simple rhythmic actions, such as marching, skipping or walking, to the music.
• Children can listen to sounds made by different pieces of percussion like the drum and the cymbal, and express these in movement. Match movement to sounds made when the percussion is played faster, slower, louder or quieter.

Using the ideas in the book

Although the ideas found here focus mainly on physical development, there are several links which can be teased out to enhance their cross-curricular potential. The links need to be made explicit either in the way a task is planned, presented and developed, or in the way the physical activity can grow out of or lead into other curricular work. These are detailed by chapter.

Chapter two

Wheeled toys
• Road safety education.
• Making work harder or easier.
• Topic work on 'people who help us': firecrew, police, ambulance service.

Chapter three

My catch game
• Designing and making.
• Communication skills, with children describing their game accuately to a partner for them to play.
• Including number patterns,1...2...1...2.

Chapter four

Treacle
• Experiencing forces to start off running and then stop under control.
• Improving stamina with longer periods of running.
• Children describing how their body feels after exercise.

Chapter five

Take a 'photograph'
• Arranging body parts around a centre of gravity.
• Shapes in stillness, extended into artwork, drawing, painting and model making.
• Making 'mirrored photos' with a partner.

Chapter six

Action Stations
• Looking at different muscles which are used at each 'action station', for development of strength.
• Problem solving, moving across each piece of apparatus using different parts of the body. For example hands and feet on benches, sideways action along a mat.
• Following instructions from word/picture cards placed by each station.

Chapter seven

Balloons
• Watching and touching the balloons and describing their properties.
• Responding to form and texture in movement.
• Expressing how it feels to move in different ways, like slowly, lightly, quietly.

Chapter eight

Broad jump
• Measuring, comparing, marking length of jump.
• Experiencing forces acting on the body as feet push hard against floor to make the body move.
• Co-operative working, observing and marking accurately.

Resources

Fixed outdoor equipment

A climbing frame, different shapes available, for example, igloo, arch, spiral staircase; Safety tiles; Playground bark; Slide; Blocks or tree stumps.

Portable outdoor equipment

Portable house/gym; Safety mats; A-frame climber with platform; Bridge ladders; Planks; Balance bars; Poles; Slide; Rocker for 1-3 children; Steps; Construction units; Barrel; Pallets; Play tunnel; Cleaned and prepared tyres; See-saw; Ropes and tubes; Rebounder; Scooter cart; Nursery cart; Bicycles; Tricycles; Wheelbarrows; Crates, boxes, hollow blocks; Natural materials, pebbles, water, sand; Buckets; Some of the above could be used indoors depending on the space available.

Small equipment for indoor or outdoor play

Balls
Choose balls with inflatable valves where possible; Ball inflator.
Large, 20cm plastic, foam or polyurethane coated foam, cloth covered.
Medium, 12-15cm plastic, foam or polyurethane coated form.
Small, 7-9cm plastic, airflow, glowballs, tennis balls, normal and low compression, sponge rubber, foam or polyurethane coated foam.
Others 'Softy' soccer, rugby, basketball balls; Large, light floater balls; Large, 'soft touch' balls; Textured balls.

Bats
Short handled, light with large hitting surface, wooden, or plastic tennis type; Miniature cricket bats, wooden cut out shapes or moulded plastic; Miniature hockey sticks, wooden cut out shapes, plastic or traditional construction.

Other small equipment
Hoops 60-90cm; Bean bags; Quoits; Shuttles; Cones 30-90cm; Polypropylene or bamboo jumping canes, 0.9m-1.5m; Activity skittles 0.6m-1.07m; Soft skittles and ball; Foam dice; Playground/field markers – cones or domes; Skipping ropes 1.8m-2.7m, long rope 3.65m.

Other useful items
Coloured baskets or storage crates; Nets for storing and carrying large balls; Blocks of coloured playground chalk; Coloured team braids; Measuring tapes 20m, 30m; Stopwatch.

Gymnastic equipment
Foldaway fixed climbing equipment, versatile with different patterns and positions, ideally with climbing ropes attached; Portable climbing and bridging equipment; Fixed or folding trestles 0.6m-1.5m high; Poles, single and double; Planks, padded and unpadded; Ladders; Floor balance bars; Padded nesting agility tables 0.45m-0.9m high; Balance benches 1.8m-2.7m; Mats, 22 or 32mm thickness. Size 1.2m x 0.9m or 1.8 x 1.2m; Geometric shaped mats; Softplay – various shapes and sizes available, barrels, bridges, cuboids, wedges, rings, cylinders, mats.

Musical equipment
Audio equipment with a counter; A selection of recorded action rhymes and music, short blank tapes; A hand drum or tambour; A tambourine; A triangle; Cymbals; Maracas; Castanets; Hand bells; Indian bells; Chime bars; Guiro; Claves; Bamboo rasp and scraper; Woodblock; Hard and soft beaters.

Planning a unit of work for P.E. see page 7

Activity area	Unit focus		Total time
Previous experience	Cross-curricular links	Resources	
Learning objectives/ outcomes	Activities	Organisation/teaching style	Assessment

Planning a session of P.E. see page 18

Activity	Unit focus	Session	Resources	Teaching focus	Teaching style, organisation, observation/ demonstration	Individual responses	Evaluation – further planning
Learning objectives/ outcomes							
Pupil activities							
Introduction							
Main activities							
Conclusion							

Some ideas for permanent playground markings, see page 29

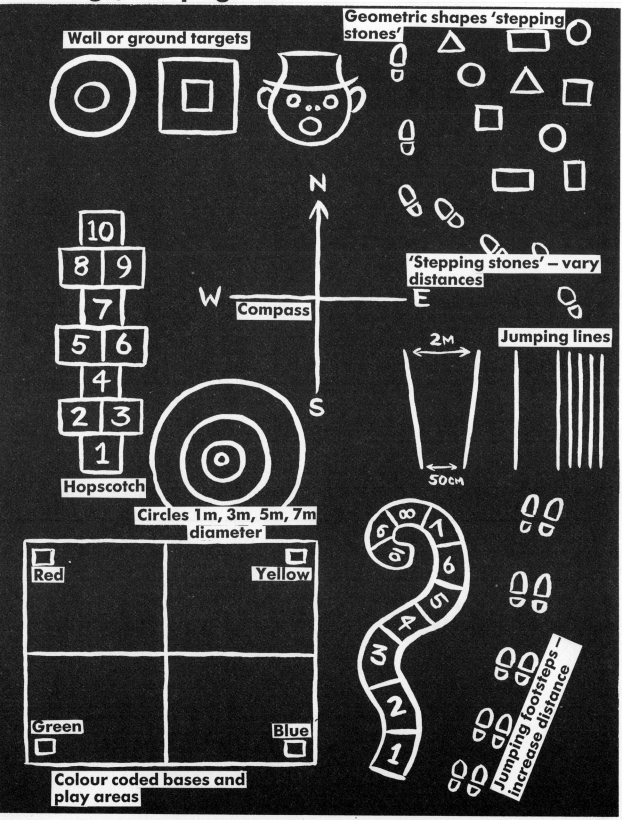

Wall or ground targets

Geometric shapes 'stepping stones'

10
8 9
7
5 6
4
2 3
1

Hopscotch

Compass

N
W E
S

'Stepping stones' – vary distances

Jumping lines

2M

50CM

Circles 1m, 3m, 5m, 7m diameter

Red   Yellow

Green   Blue

Colour coded bases and play areas

8 7
9
10 6
5
4
3
2
1

Jumping footsteps – increase distance

Useful addresses

Advisory Centre for Education (ACE),
18 Victoria Park Square,
London E2 9PB

British Association for
Early Childhood Education,
111 City View House,
463 Bethnal Green Road,
London E2 9QH

Pre-School Playgroups Association,
61-63 Kings Cross Road,
London WC1X 9LL

Scottish Pre-School Playgroups
Association,
14 Elliot Place,
Glasgow G3 8EP

Tutors of Advanced Courses for
Teachers of Young Children (TACTYC),
BCM,
PO Box 5342,
London WC1N 3XX

High/Scope UK,
Research and Development Section,
Barnardo's,
Tanner's Lane,
Barkingside,
Ilford,
Essex IG6 1QG

The National Association of
Special Educational Needs (NASEN),
2 Lichfield Road,
Stafford ST17 4JX

Health Education Authority,
Hamilton House,
Mabledon Place,
London WC1X 9TX

Health Education Authority Group
for Scotland,
Woodburn House,
Canaan Lane,
Edinburgh EH10 4SG

National Children's Play and
Recreation Unit,
359/361 Euston Road (First Floor),
London NW1 3AL

Physical Education Association of
Great Britain and Northern Ireland
(P.E.A.),
Ling House,
5 Western Court,
Bromley Street,
Digbeth,
Birmingham B9 4AN

Sports Council,
16 Upper Woburn Place,
London WC1H 0QP

Scottish Sports Council,
Caledonia House,
South Gyle,
Edinburgh EH12 9DQ

Royal Society for the Prevention of
Accidents (RoSPA),
Cannon House,
The Priory,
Queensway,
Birmingham B4 6BS